W9-ATK-973

EXOCET

The weapon—a low flying atomic missile invisible to radar—that one nation would kill anyone to get and another nation would stop at nothing to protect.

EXOCET

The prize in a savagely violent hot-and-cold war game that stretched from the Falklands to Paris to a besieged Channel Island fortress.

EXOCET

The magnet that drew a ruthless English undercover agent, a gallant Argentine air ace, a master Soviet spy, and the exquisite beauty they all wanted into a passionate, perilous, whirlpool of desire, deceit, and double-dealing . . . and forced the most difficult choice a woman in love ever had to make. . . .

"SUPERIOR . . . SPECTACULAR . . . SOMETHING HAPPENS EVERY MINUTE TO KEEP THE READER TURNING THE PAGES."

The Best in Fiction from SIGNET

EXOCET

JACK HIGGINS

A SIGNET BOOK
NEW AMERICAN LIBRARY

To Denise
For love, understanding, and grace

Publisher's Note

This novel is a work of fiction. Names, characters, places, and incidents are either the product of the author's imagination or are used fictitiously, and any resemblance to actual persons, living or dead, events, or locales is entirely coincidental.

SIGNET TRADEMARK REG. U.S. PAT. OFF. AND FOREIGN COUNTRIES
REGISTERED TRADEMARK—MARCA REGISTRADA
HECHO EN CHICAGO, U.S.A.

SIGNET, SIGNET CLASSIC, MENTOR, PLUME, MERIDIAN and NAL BOOKS
are published by New American Library,
1633 Broadway, New York, New York 10019

First Signet Printing, July, 1984

1 2 3 4 5 6 7 8 9

PRINTED IN THE UNITED STATES OF AMERICA

1

As the yellow Telecoms truck turned the corner, Grosvenor Place was quiet in the rain, not another vehicle in sight, hardly surprising in view of the weather and the fact that it was three o'clock in the morning.

Harvey Jackson reduced speed, his hands slippery with sweat as he gripped the wheel. He wore yellow oilskins, a large man in his late thirties, the dark hair long, framing a face that seldom smiled, the eyes bleak above high cheekbones.

The rain was so heavy that the windshield wipers had difficulty in handling it. He pulled in at the curb and took a cigarette from a packet in the dashboard. He lit it and wound down the window, looking across the road at the high perimeter wall topped with barbed wire that enclosed the gardens at the rear of Buckingham Palace.

He rapped with his knuckles against the partition

behind him. A panel opened instantly and Villiers peered out. "Yes?"

"We're here. Are you ready?"

"Two minutes. Get us into position."

The panel was closed and Jackson moved into gear and drove away.

The interior of the truck was crowded with the paraphernalia of the telephone engineer and brightly lit by a neon strip light. Tony Villiers braced himself against the workbench as the truck swayed and carefully blacked his face with camouflage cream, observing the effect in a mirror propped up against a toolbox.

He was perhaps thirty and of medium height with good shoulders. The eyes were dark and quite without expression. At some time or other his nose had been broken. His hair was black and tangled and almost shoulder length. The black jumpsuit and French paratrooper's boots he wore combined to make him look a thoroughly dangerous man.

And there was a kind of weary bitterness to him, as well, a look about the face of someone who had got to know the world and its inhabitants too well and did not care for what he had found.

He pulled a black woolen hood over his head, leaving only his eyes free, and grabbed at the bench as the truck swung across the road, mounted the pavement, and pulled in beside the wall.

A Smith & Wesson magnum revolver with a Carswell silencer screwed on to the barrel lay on the bench beside a briefcase. He slipped it into the pouch on his right leg, opened the briefcase and took out a large black and white photograph. It had been taken late on the previous afternoon with a telephoto lens and showed the Ambassador's Entrance at the side of Buckingham Palace. There were workmen's ladders against the wall and under the portico. More important, two or three windows above the flat roof were partially open.

Villiers replaced the photograph and opened the panel again. "Twenty-five minutes, Harvey. If I'm not back, get the hell out of it."

"Conversation I don't need, not on a night like this," Jackson said. "Just get it done so we can go home."

Villiers closed the panel, clambered up on the bench, and opened a trap. He pulled himself up on the roof and closed the trap behind him, crouching there in the rain. The wall was only a couple of yards away. He slipped across the barbed wire, grabbed for the branch of a tree, worked his way along it, hand over hand, then dropped into the darkness below.

The police officer on security duties at the Grosvenor Place end of the palace gardens that morning was thoroughly unhappy with life. Soaked to the skin, wet and miserable, he had paused to shelter under a tree when the Alsatian at his side whined softly.

"What is it, boy?" he demanded, instantly alert, and slipped the lead. "Seek, boy! Seek!"

The Alsatian departed silently, but Villiers, standing beside a tree twenty or thirty-yards away, was already alerted by that first whine and reached for the aerosol spray he carried in another pouch of his jumpsuit. The dog, specially trained to silent attack, launched itself at him, and his left arm, padded against just such a situation, swung up. The Alsatian chewed savagely at the quilted material, and Villiers sprayed the aerosol into its face. The animal collapsed without a sound and lay still.

A moment later, the police officer approached cautiously. "Rex, where are you, boy?"

Villiers's hand rose and fell against the back of the neck in one sharp, practiced blow. The police officer groaned and keeled over. Villiers pinioned him, hands behind his back, with his own handcuffs and took the officer's radio receiver from his pocket and slipped it into another pouch of his jumpsuit. Then he started to run across the park through the darkness toward the rear of the palace.

Harvey Jackson got out of the truck and opened the door. He reached inside, found a couple of grappling hooks, then bent down over the telephone manhole at his feet and removed it. He took from the truck an inspection lamp on a long cord, which he lowered into the darkness, a red warning sign reading: DANGER, MEN AT WORK, some canvas screens, and an awning. He dropped into the manhole, opened one of the inspection boxes, revealing a bewildering array of multicolored wires and switches, and sat back and waited.

Perhaps five minutes later, there was the sound

of a car, and he stood up and peered over the edge as a police patrol car pulled in at the curb. The driver leaned out, a grin on his face.

"What a way to earn a living. Serves you right for joining."

"You, too," Jackson said.

"Hope you're getting double time, this hour of the bloody morning."

"That'll be the day."

The policeman grinned again. "Watch yourself. If this rain keeps up you'll be swimming in there by breakfast time."

He drove away, and Jackson lit a cigarette and sat down again, whistling softly to himself, wondering how Villiers was getting on.

And Villiers, who had found the workmen's ladders still available under the portico, had reached the flat roof over the Ambassador's Entrance with no difficulty. Two of the windows in the photograph were still partially open. He worked his way along a ledge, raised the nearest one, and slid over the windowsill into a small office. He opened the door cautiously and slipped out into a dark corridor.

The Royal Apartments were on the other side of the palace. Completely familiar with the layout from his study of the plans supplied to him, he now moved with considerable rapidity through a maze of corridors, all deserted as he had expected at that time of the morning. Some five minutes later he stood at the end of the corridor leading to the private quarters.

The Queen's apartment was only a few yards away—a dining room leading into a sitting room, the bedroom beyond, he knew. Farther on, around another corner, was a room where the corgis slept. In the page's vestibule opposite, a police constable sat reading a paperback book.

Villiers observed him carefully for a moment, then retreated down the corridor and took out the radio transceiver he had taken from the policeman in the park. He pressed the channel 4 button and waited.

There was a slight crackle. A voice said, "Jones here."

Villiers said in a soft voice, "Security office. The picture gallery alarm seems to be playing up again. We're getting an intermittent signal. Give it a quick check, will you?"

"Okay," Jones said.

Villiers moved to the corner again and peered around in time to see the police constable moving away along the corridor in the other direction. He turned at the end and disappeared. Villiers moved instantly to the door of the Queen's apartment. He paused for a moment, took a deep breath and opened it.

Her Majesty, Queen Elizabeth the Second, was seated by the fire in her comfortable sitting room reading a book. In spite of the early hour, she was perfectly groomed and wore a pale blue sweater set and tweed skirt, pearls at her throat. A slight creaking from the door caused her to raise her head. It opened and Villiers stepped into the room, closing the door behind him.

He looked supremely menacing in the black jump-suit and hood, only the eyes showing. There was silence for a moment and then he reached up and pulled the hood over his head.

"Ah, Major Villiers," the Queen said. "Was it difficult?"

"I'm afraid not, ma'am."

The Queen frowned. "I see. Well, we'd better get on with it. You are on limited time, I presume?"

"Very, ma'am."

She reached for a newspaper and held it up. "Last night's *Evening Standard*. Will that do?"

"I think so, ma'am."

Villiers took a folding Polaroid camera from one of the pouches in his jumpsuit, moved close, and dropped to one knee. The Queen raised the newspaper, there was a flash, and he took the picture, a soft whirring as it was discharged from the camera. He moved to the fire and held the photo to the warmth, and her face started to appear.

"Excellent, ma'am." He held it out to her.

"Good, then you'd better be off. Wouldn't do for them to catch you now. That really would spoil everything."

Villiers pulled the hood back over his head and gave her a slight bow. The door clicked behind him and he was gone. The Queen sat there for a while, thinking about it, debating whether to go to bed. Rain drummed against the window. She shivered, picked up the book, and returned to her reading.

Ten minutes later, Tony Villiers came over the wall like a black wraith and landed on the roof of the Telecoms truck.

"Let's move it, Harvey," he whispered, as he opened the trapdoor and dropped down onto the bench.

Jackson was out of the manhole in an instant, had the door open and passed in the canvas screens, the awning, the warning sign, and the lamp and closed the door again. Villiers heard the manhole clang into place, footsteps hurry around to the cab. He pulled off his hood, opened a jar of theatrical cleansing cream, and started on his face. A moment later, they drove away.

In 1972, the problem of international terrorism having reached epidemic proportions, the Director-General of DI5, the British Secret Intelligence Service, authorized the setting up within the organization of a section known as Group Four, whose powers derived directly from the Prime Minister, to coordinate the handling of all cases of terrorism, subversion, and the like.

Brigadier Charles Ferguson had been placed in charge, still was, a large, kindly looking man whose crumpled suits always seemed a size too large. The

Guards tie was his only military aspect. The untidy gray hair and double chin combined to give him the appearance of some minor professor.

Just now, he wore a greatcoat of the type favored by officers of the Household Brigade, the collar turned up against the early morning cold. The Bentley was parked off Eaton Square, not too far from the palace, and the only other occupant was the driver, Harry Fox, a slim, elegant man of twenty-nine who until three years previously had been an acting captain in the Blues and Royals. The neat leather glove he wore on the left hand concealed the fact that he had lost the original in a bomb explosion during a tour of duty in Belfast.

He poured tea from a Thermos flask into plastic cups and handed Ferguson one. "I wonder how he's getting on?"

"Our Tony? Oh, with his usual appallingly ruthless efficiency. Never lets anything get in his way, you see. Comes of having been a prefect at Eton."

"Nevertheless, sir, if he's caught, it will raise one hell of a stink, and it won't do the SIS image much good either."

"You worry too much, Harry," Ferguson said. "Comes of having picked up the wrong briefcase over there. Things could be worse." He nodded across the square to a yellow Telecoms truck parked beside an open manhole, canvas screen around it. Two men in yellow oilskins worked in the rain. "Just look at those two poor sods. What a way to earn your bread. Down a hole at this ungodly hour in the morning in the pouring rain."

A dark Ford Granada passed them, one man at the wheel, another in the rear. It pulled in at the curb and a large bulky man in a dark raincoat and trilby hat came toward them, opened the rear door, and got in.

"Ah, Superintendent," Ferguson said. "Harry, this is Detective Chief Superintendent Carver of Special Branch, delegated by the powers that be at Scotland Yard to be official observer this morning. You should beware, Superintendent." Ferguson filled another plastic cup with tea and offered it to him. "In the old days, messengers who brought bad news were usually executed."

"Balls," Carver said amiably. "He doesn't stand a chance, your man, and you know it. How did he intend to try and get in anyway?"

"I haven't the slightest idea," Ferguson told him. "I never query methods, Superintendent, only results."

"Just a minute, sir," Fox said. "I think we've got company."

The two telephone engineers who had been working in the manhole at the far side of the square had got out and were walking toward them, oilskins streaming with rain. Fox opened the glove compartment and took out a Walther PPK.

Ferguson said, "How enterprising of them," and wound down the window. "Good morning, Tony. Morning, Sergeant Major."

"Sir," Jackson said, bringing his heels together automatically.

Villiers leaned down and passed in the Polaroid photo of the Queen. "Anything else, sir?" he asked.

Ferguson examined the photo without a word, then passed it to the Superintendent. Carver sat up straight. "Good God."

Ferguson took the photo from him, produced a lighter and touched it to the edge. He passed it to Villiers. "Wouldn't do to have that floating around. Better tell us the worst."

Villiers held the photo as it burned. "The alarm beam directly inside the grounds is positioned only two feet from the wall. No problem in jumping over that. At the palace itself, the alarm system is in some cases old-fashioned or faulty. And to get in, you don't need to be a cat burglar." He passed over the photo taken the previous day. "Workmen leave ladders, housemaids leave windows open—it's a farce."

Carver studied the photo glumly. Villiers said, "We'll take a walk. Leave you to it, sir."

He and Jackson walked to the nearest lamp and lit cigarettes. Carver said, "Who is he, for Christ's sake? He talks like the Cavalry Club and looks like some East End hood."

"Actually he's a major in the Grenadier Guards attached to the SAS," Ferguson said.

"With that hair? I mean, look at it."

"Special dispensation in the SAS, going without haircuts. Personal camouflage is very important, Superintendent, if you're trying to pass yourself off as some back-street yobbo on the Belfast docks."

"And he's reliable?"

"Oh, yes. Decorated twice. Military Cross for action against Marxist guerrillas in the Oman and another for some nonsense or other in Ireland, details not for release."

Carver held up the photo. "This is bad. There will be hell to pay."

"We'll send you a full report."

"I bet you will."

Carver got out of the car and Villiers turned and came toward him, his face pale in the street light.

"One thing I didn't mention, Superintendent. Your man on prowler guard at the Grosvenor Place end of the Palace Gardens. I had to belt him. You'll find him under a tree by the pond in his own handcuffs. He's okay. I checked him out on the way back. Tell him I'm sorry about the dog."

"You bastard!" Carver said.

He hurried along to the Granada, the door slammed, it drove away.

Ferguson said, "Get in, Tony. I presume you can be relied upon to get rid of that truck, Sergeant Major? I won't inquire where it came from."

"Sir." Jackson clicked his heels and moved off across the square.

Villiers got into the Bentley beside Ferguson and Fox drove away. Ferguson said, "You've another week of your leave to go?"

"Officially."

Ferguson wound down the window and peered out as they rounded the Queen Victoria Memorial at the front of the palace and went down the mall.

"Have you seen Gabrielle lately?"

Villiers said calmly, "No."

"Is she still at the flat in Kensington Palace Gardens?"

"Some of the time. That one belongs to me. She uses it by arrangement. She has her place in Paris, of course."

"I was sorry to hear about the divorce."

"Don't be," Villiers said flatly. "The best thing that ever happened to both of us."

"You really mean that?"

"Oh, yes."

Ferguson shivered and pulled the collar of his coat up around his neck and yet he lowered the window even more so that the cold morning air rushed in.

"Sometimes I wonder what life's all about."

"Well, don't ask me," Villiers told him. "I'm only passing through."

He folded his arms, leaned back in the corner, closed his eyes, and was instantly asleep.

2

Brigadier Charles Ferguson preferred to work when possible from his Cavendish Square flat. It was his especial joy. The Adam fireplace was real and so was the fire that burned there. The rest was Georgian also. Everything matched to perfection, including the curtains. He was sitting by the fire at ten o'clock on the morning after Villiers's exploit at the palace, reading the *Financial Times,* when the door opened and his manservant, Kim, an ex-Gurkha *naik* appeared.

"Mademoiselle Legrand, sir."

Ferguson removed his half-moon reading glasses, put them down with the paper, and stood up. "Show her in, Kim, and tea for three, please."

Kim departed, and a moment later Gabrielle Legrand entered the room.

She was, as always, Ferguson told himself, the most strikingly beautiful woman he had ever seen in his life. She was dressed for riding in boots, faded jodhpurs, white shirt, and an old green jacket in

Donegal tweed. The blonde hair was held back from the forehead by a scarlet band and rolled up into a bun at the nape of the neck. She regarded him gravely, the wide green eyes giving nothing away, the riding crop she carried in her left hand tapping her knee. She was not small, almost five foot eight in her boots that morning. Ferguson went toward her with a smile of conscious pleasure, hands outstretched.

"My lovely Gabrielle." He kissed her cheek. "No longer Mrs. Villiers, I see?"

"No," she said flatly. "I'm me again."

Her voice was pleasantly English upper class, but with its own timbre that gave it a unique quality. She dropped her crop on the table, went to the window, and peered down into the square.

"Have you seen Tony lately?"

"I should have thought you would have," Ferguson said. "He's in town. Spot of leave, as I understand it. Hasn't he called at the flat?"

"No," she said. "He wouldn't do that, not while I'm there."

She stayed at the window and Ferguson said gently, "What went wrong between you two, my love?"

"Everything," she said. "And nothing. We thought we were in love one long hot summer five years ago. I was beautiful, he was the best looking thing in a uniform I ever saw."

"And then?"

"We didn't jell—never did. The chemistry was all wrong." The voice was flat calm and yet he sensed distress there. "I cared for Tony, still do, but I got

angry with him too easily and I never knew why."
She shrugged again. "Too many spaces we could never fill."

"I'm sorry," Ferguson said.

The door opened and Kim entered with a silver tray, which he placed by the fire. "Ah, tea," Ferguson said. "Get Captain Fox from the office, Kim."

The Gurkha went out and Gabrielle sat down by the fire. Ferguson sat opposite and poured tea into a china cup for her.

She drank a little and smiled. "Excellent. The English half of me approves."

"Filthy stuff, coffee," he told her.

He offered her a cigarette. She shook her head. "No thanks, I'd prefer to get down to business. I have a luncheon appointment. What do you want?"

At that moment the door opened and Harry Fox came in. He wore a Guards tie and a light gray flannel suit and carried a file, which he placed on the desk.

"Gabrielle, how nice." He was genuinely pleased and leaned down to kiss her cheek.

"Harry." She patted his face affectionately. "What's he up to now?"

Fox took the cup of tea Ferguson offered and looked at him inquiringly. Ferguson nodded and the young captain stood by the fire and carried on.

"What do you know about the Falkland Islands, Gabrielle?"

"In the South Atlantic," she said. "About four hundred miles off the Argentine coast. The Argentine government has been claiming them for years."

"That's right. British sovereign territory, of course, but a lousy place to defend eight thousand miles away."

"As a matter of interest," Ferguson said, "we have sixty-eight Royal Marines in the islands at the moment, backed up by the local defense force and one ship of the Royal Navy—HMS *Endurance*, an ice patrol vessel, armed with two 20-mm guns and a couple of Wasp helicopters. Our masters in Parliament have been making it clear in public debate that they intend to scrap her to save money."

"And just four hundred miles away is a superbly equipped air force, a large army, and a navy," Fox said.

Gabrielle shrugged. "So what? You're not seriously suggesting that the Argentine government would invade?"

"I'm afraid that's exactly what we *are* suggesting," Ferguson said. "All the signs have pointed that way since January, and the C.I.A. certainly think it's on the cards. It makes a lot of sense. The country is run by a three-man junta. The President, General Galtieri, who is also Commander-in-Chief of the Army, has a commitment to economic recovery. Unfortunately, the country is almost bankrupt."

Fox said, "An invasion of the Falklands would prove a very welcome diversion. Take the people's minds off other things."

"Just like the Romans," Ferguson said. "Bread and circuses. Keep the mob happy. Another cup?"

He poured Gabrielle more tea. She said, "I still don't see where I come into this."

"Very simple, really."

Ferguson nodded to Fox, who opened the file on the desk and took out an ornate invitation card, which he passed to her. In English and Spanish, His Excellency Carlos Ortiz de Rozas, Argentine Ambassador to the Court of St. James's, invited Mademoiselle Gabrielle Simone Legrand to a cocktail party and buffet, seven-thirty for eight, at the Argentine Embassy in Wilton Crescent.

"Just off Belgrave Square," Fox said helpfully.

"This evening?" she said. "Impossible. I'm going to the theater."

"This one's important, Gabrielle." Ferguson nodded and Fox got the file, opened it, and took out a black and white photograph, which he put on the table in front of her.

Gabrielle picked it up. The man who stared out at her wore a military flying suit of the kind used by jet pilots. He carried a flying helmet in his right hand, and there was a scarf at his throat. He was not young, at least forty, and like most pilots he was not particularly tall. He had dark wavy hair, graying a little at the temples, and calm eyes. There was a scar on his right cheek, running up into the eye.

"Colonel Raul Carlos Montera," Fox said. "Special air attaché at the Embassy at the present time."

Gabrielle stared down at the photo. It was like looking at an old friend, someone she knew well, and yet she had never seen this man before in her life.

"Tell me about him."

"Age forty-five," Fox said. "An aristocrat. His

23

mother, Donna Elena, is very much a leader of society in Buenos Aires. His father died last year. Family owns God knows how much land and all the cows in the world. Very rich."

"And he's a pilot?"

"Oh yes, of the obsessional kind. Soloed at sixteen. He did a languages degree at Harvard, then joined the Argentine Air Force. Trained with the RAF at Cranwell. Has also trained with the South Africans and Israelis."

"Important point," Ferguson said, moving to the window. "Not your usual South American fascist. In 1967 he resigned his commission. Flew Dakotas for the Biafrans during the Nigerian civil war. Night flights from Fernando Po to Port Harcourt. Rather a bad scene.

"Then he joined up with a Swedish aristocrat, Count Carl Gustaf von Rosen. The Biafrans bought five Swedish training planes called Minicons. Had them fixed up with machine guns and so on. Montera was one of those crazy enough to fly them against Russian MIG fighters piloted by Egyptians and East Germans." Fox passed her another photo. "Taken in Port Harcourt, just before the end of the war."

He wore an old World War Two leather flying jacket, his hair was tousled, the eyes shadowed, the face drawn with fatigue. The scar on his cheek looked raised and angry, as if fresh. She wanted to reach out and comfort him, this man she didn't even know. When she put the photograph down, her hand shook slightly.

"What exactly am I supposed to do?"

"He'll be there tonight," Ferguson said. "Let's face it, Gabrielle, few men can resist you at the best of times, but when you take special pains . . ."

The sentence hung in mid-air, unfinished. She said, "I see. I'm to take him to bed, lie back, think of England, and hope he says something worth hearing about the Falklands?"

"Put rather starkly, but close enough."

"What a bastard you are, Charles." She got up and picked up her riding crop.

"Will you do it?" he asked.

"I think so," she said. "I've seen the play before anyway and to be honest, this Raul Montera of yours looks much more interesting." The door closed behind her.

Fox poured himself more tea. "You think she'll do it, sir?"

"Oh yes," Ferguson said. "She loves to take part in the theater of life, our Gabrielle. How much do you know about her background, Harry?"

"Well, she and Tony were married for what, five years?"

"That's right. French father and English mother. They were divorced when she was quite young. She read politics and economics at the Sorbonne, then did a year at St. Hugh's at Oxford. Married Villiers after meeting him at a Cambridge May Ball. Should have known better than attend a function at a second-rate university. How many times has she worked for us, Harry?"

"Only once where I've had direct contact, sir. Four other occasions through you."

"Yes," Ferguson said. "A truly brilliant linguist. No good where the rough stuff is concerned, either physical or anything else. A genuine moralist, our Gabrielle. What family has she got living now?"

"Father in Marseilles. Her mother, sir, and stepfather. He's English. They live in the Isle of Wight. She has a half brother, Richard, aged twenty-two, serving as a helicopter pilot in the Royal Navy."

Ferguson lit a cigar and sat behind the desk. "I've met women, Harry, and so have you, of beauty and considerable distinction, but Gabrielle is something quite unique. Quite special, and for a woman like that, only a very special man will do."

"I think we're fresh out of those this year, sir," Fox said.

"We usually are, Harry. We usually are. Now let's go through the Foreign Office tray." Ferguson put on his half-moon spectacles.

3

The scene in the ballroom at the Argentine Embassy was really quite splendid, crystal chandeliers taking light to every corner, reflected again in the mirrored walls. Beautiful women, exquisitely gowned, handsome men, dress uniforms, an occasional church dignitary in scarlet and purple. It was all rather archaic, as if somehow the mirrors were reflecting a dim memory of long ago, the dancers turning endlessly to faint music.

The trio playing on a raised dais in one corner were really rather good and the music was exactly the kind Raul Montera liked. All the old favorites. Cole Porter, Rodgers and Hart, Irving Berlin. And yet he was bored. He excused himself from the small group around the Ambassador, took a glass of Perrier water from the tray carried by a passing waiter, and leaned negligently against a pillar, smoking a cigarette.

His face was pale, the eyes a vivid blue, constantly

in motion in spite of his apparent calmness. The elegant dress uniform fitted him to perfection, the medals making a brave show on his left breast. There was an energy to him, an eager restlessness that seemed to say he found such affairs trivial and longed for something more active.

The major-domo's voice rose above the hubbub. "Mademoiselle Gabrielle Legrand." Montera glanced up casually and saw her standing in the entrance, reflected in the gilt mirror in front of him.

It was as if the breath went out of him for a moment. He stood there, transfixed, then turned slowly to look at the most beautiful woman he had ever seen in his life.

Her hair was no longer banded and gathered up as it had been that morning at Ferguson's office; it really was one of her most astonishing features. Very blonde and cut in the French style known as *Le Coupe Sauvage*. Long enough to hang between the shoulder blades, yet apparently short at the front, layered and feathered at the sides, framing a face of considerable beauty.

The eyes were the most vivid green, the high cheekbones gave her a Scandinavian look, and the mouth was wide and beautifully formed. She was wearing an evening dress in silver thread and tambour beading, the uneven hemline well above the knee, for the mini had returned to fashion that season. She balanced on silver high-heeled shoes, carrying herself with a touch of arrogance that seemed to say *Take me or leave me, I couldn't care less,* as she surveyed the room calmly.

Raul Montera had never seen any woman in his life who looked more capable of taking on the whole world if she had to. And she, in her turn, had seen him, and conscious of a strange, irrational excitement, turned away as if looking for someone.

She was immediately accosted by a young army captain who was obviously slightly the worse for drink. Montera gave him enough time to make a thorough nuisance of himself, then moved through the crowd to her side.

"Ah, there you are, cherie," he said in excellent French. "I've been looking everywhere for you."

Her reflexes were excellent. She turned smoothly, reached up and kissed him on the cheek. "I was beginning to wonder if I'd got the wrong night."

"At your orders, my colonel." The young army captain retired in confusion. Montera looked at Gabrielle wryly and they both burst into laughter.

He took her hands and held them lightly. "You get a lot of that, I suppose?"

"Since I was about fourteen."

There was a shadow in the green eyes. He said, "Which has not improved your opinion of my sex, I think?"

"If you mean, do I like men, no, not very much." She smiled. "In the generality, that is."

He examined her hands. "Ah, good."

"What is?" She was puzzled.

29

"No wedding ring."

He drew himself up and clicked his heels together. "Colonel Raul Carlos Montera, very much at your orders, and I would consider it a privilege and a joy to secure not only this dance, but every other available this evening."

He took her hand and drew her on to the floor as the trio started to play in slow foxtrot tempo "Our Love Is Here to Stay."

"How remarkably appropriate," he said and drew her to him.

And to that, there could be no answer. They danced well together, his arm holding her lightly around the waist.

She touched the scar on his cheek. "How did you get that?"

"Cannon shell splinter," he said. "Aerial combat."

She played her part well. "But when? Argentina hasn't been to war in my lifetime."

"Another man's war," he said. "A thousand years ago. Too long a story."

She touched the scar again gently and he groaned and said in Spanish to himself, "I've heard of love at first sight but this is ridiculous."

"Why?" she replied calmly in the same language. "Isn't it what the poets for centuries now have been assuring us is the only kind worth having?"

"Spanish as well?" he demanded. "Is there no end to this woman's marvels?"

"Also English," she said. "And German. My Russian isn't fluent, though. Only passable."

"Amazing."

"You mean, for a beautiful blonde with a good body?"

There was bitterness in her voice, and he moved back to look into her face. There was genuine tenderness in his own and a kind of authority.

"If I have hurt you, forgive me. It was not intended. I will learn, though, to mend my manners. You must give me time."

And there was that breathlessness in her again as the music stopped and he drew her off the floor. "Champagne?" he said. "Being French I would presume it to be your drink."

"But of course."

He snapped his fingers to a waiter, took a glass from the proffered tray and handed it to her. "Dom Perignon—only the best. We're trying to make friends and influence people tonight."

"I should imagine you'd need to," she said.

He frowned. "I don't understand."

"Oh, there was an item on the television news earlier this evening. Questions in the British Parliament about the Falklands. Apparently your Navy is about to go on maneuvers in the area."

"Not the Falklands," he said. "To us, the Malvinas." He shrugged. "An old quarrel, but not worth arguing about. The politicians have it in hand. In my opinion, the British will probably do a deal with us in the not too distant future."

She let it go, slipped a hand in his arm and they crossed to an open French window and moved out.

On the way, he picked another glass of champagne off a passing tray for her.

"Don't you drink?" she asked.

"Not a great deal and certainly not champagne. It creates havoc with me. I'm getting old, you see."

"Nonsense."

"Forty-five. And you?"

"Twenty-seven."

"Dear God, that I should be so young again."

"Age," she said, "is a state of mind. Herman Hesse said somewhere that in reality, youth and age exist only among ordinary people. All more talented and exceptional people are sometimes young and sometimes old, just as they are sometimes happy and sometimes sad."

"Such wisdom," he said. "Where does it all come from?"

"I went to the Sorbonne and then Oxford," she said. "A woman's college, St. Hugh's. Not a man in sight and thank God for it."

Behind them the trio started to play "A Foggy Day in London Town." "I was a stranger in your city . . ." He started to sing the intro softly in English.

"Oh no," she said. "Paris is my city, but Fred Astaire had it right in the movie when he sang that song. Everyone should walk along the Thames Embankment at least once, preferably after midnight."

He smiled slowly and held her hands. "An excellent idea. But first, we eat. You look like a woman with an appetite. A little more champagne and then, who knows?"

It was raining hard and fog crouched at the end of the streets. The trenchcoat he had found for her was soaked, as was the scarf she had bound around her hair. Montera was still in uniform, his magnificence anonymous under a heavy officer's greatcoat, and he wore a peaked cap.

They had walked for several miles in the pouring rain followed by his official car, a patient chauffeur at the wheel. She wore a pair of flat shoes he had borrowed for her from one of the maids at the Embassy.

Birdcage Walk, the palace, St. James's Park. Montera had never enjoyed himself in the company of another human being so much.

"Sure you haven't had enough?" he asked as they moved down toward Westminster Bridge.

"Not yet. I promised you something special, remember?"

"Ah, I was forgetting."

They came to the bridge and she turned onto the Embankment. "Well, this is it. The most romantic place in town. In that old movie, Fred Astaire would have held my arm and sung to me as we strolled with the car following us, crawling along the curb."

"Ah, but the traffic situation has changed since then, as you can see," he told her. "Too many cars parked at the curb already."

Above them, Big Ben chimed the first stroke of midnight. "The witching hour," she said. "Have you enjoyed your guided tour?"

He lit a cigarette and leaned on the parapet. "Oh yes, I like London. A wonderful town."

"But the English not so much?"

It was there again, that extraordinary perception, and he shrugged. "They're all right. I trained with the RAF at Cranwell and they were good—the best. The trouble is that to them we're all *dagos,* we South Americans, so if the *dago* is a good flyer, it's because they've done a good job on him."

"That's shit," she said, coldly angry. "They don't owe you a thing. You're a great pilot. The best."

"And how would you know that?" he asked curiously.

The rain increased into a solid drenching downpour, and he turned and whistled to the car, farther along the Embankment. "I'd better get you home."

"Yes," she said. "It would seem appropriate," and taking his hand they ran together toward the car.

The Pissarro on the wall of the sitting room of the flat in Kensington Palace Gardens was really quite beautiful. Montera, standing before it, a brandy in his hand, examined it closely.

Gabrielle came out of the bedroom brushing her hair. She wore an old bathrobe, a man's obviously, several sizes too big for her.

Montera said, "Do my eyes deceive me or is the Pissarro an original?"

"My father, I'm afraid, is disgustingly wealthy," she said. "Electronics, armaments, things like that. His headquarters are in Marseilles and he tends to indulge me."

He took in the robe and said gravely, "It was too much to expect that a girl like you could have reached the ripe old age of twenty-seven without complication. You are married, I think? I was wrong."

"Divorced," she said.

"Ah, I see."

"And you?"

"My wife died four years ago. Leukemia. I was always rather difficult to please so my mother arranged things. She's like that. She was the daughter of a family friend."

"A suitable match for a Montera?"

"Exactly. I have a ten-year-old daughter named Linda who lives contentedly with her grandmother. I am not a good father. Too impatient."

"I can't believe that."

And then he was close and she was in his arms and his lips brushed her face. "I love you. Don't ask me how, but it's true. I've never known anyone like you."

He kissed her. For a moment she responded and then she pushed him away and there was something strangely like fear in her eyes.

"Please, Raul, no. Not now."

He took her hands gently and nodded. "Of course. I understand. I do, believe me. May I call you in the morning?"

"Yes, please do."

He released her, picked up his greatcoat, went to the door and opened it. He turned and smiled, a wry smile of such charm that she ran across the room and put her hands on his shoulders.

"You're so damned nice to me. I'm not used to that. Not from men. Give me time."

"All you need." He smiled again. "You made me feel so gentle. I amazed myself."

The door closed softly behind him, she leaned against it, filled with a delight that she had never known in her life before.

Outside, as soon as Montera got into the back of the Embassy car, the driver sped away. A moment later Tony Villiers stepped out of a nearby doorway. He lit a cigarette and watched the car go, then turned to look up at the windows of the flat. As he did so, the lights were turned out. He stood there for a moment longer, then turned and walked away.

Brigadier Charles Ferguson was sitting in bed, propped against pillows, working his way through a mass of papers when the red phone rang, the line that connected him directly with his office at the Directorate-General of the Security Service in the large, anonymous, white and red brick building in the West End of London, not far from the Hilton Hotel.

"Ferguson here."

Harry Fox said, "Coded message from the CIA in Washington, sir. They seem to think that the Argentinians will hit the Falklands within the next few days."

"Do they indeed? What does the Foreign Office have to say?"

"They think it's a load of cobblers, sir."

"They would, wouldn't they? Any word from Gabrielle?"

"Not yet."

"An interesting point, Harry. Raul Montera is one of the few pilots in the Argentine Air Force with genuine combat experience. If they were going to start anything, you'd think they'd recall him."

"Even cleverer to leave him in London, sir."

"That's true. Anyway, I'll see you in the morning. If we haven't heard from Gabrielle by noon I'll phone her."

He put down the receiver, picked up a file, and went back to work.

4

When Gabrielle admitted Montera the following morning, she was fresh from the bath and wearing the same robe. He was wearing jeans and an old, black leather flying jacket. He had called her at eight o'clock, unable to bear the waiting.

"You said to make it informal," he said.

She kissed him on the cheek and fingered the gold crucifix on the chain that hung around his neck. "You look gorgeous."

She had spoken in English and he replied in the same language. "Gorgeous? Is that a word to apply to a man?"

"Gorgeous," she insisted. "Stop role playing. I thought we'd go for a walk. Across Kensington Gardens and down to Harrods. I've some shopping to do."

"Fine."

He lit a cigarette and sat reading the morning paper while she went to dress. There was an account of yesterday's proceedings in Parliament and questions to the Prime Minister on the Falklands. He read the report with interest, only looking up when Gabrielle stepped back into the room.

She was an astonishing sight in a yellow T-shirt that clearly outlined her breasts, a tight white skirt that ended above the knee, and a pair of high-heeled cowboy boots. A pair of sunglasses were perched on top of her blonde hair.

"Shall we go?" she said.

"Yes, of course," he said. He stood up and opened the door for her. He smiled. "You are a woman of surprises. Did anyone ever tell you that?"

"Often," she said and moved past him.

The crowd in Kensington Gardens was remarkably cosmopolitan. Arabs and Asians of every variety mingled freely with the native British. People lounged on the grass, boys played football in the bright sunshine, and Gabrielle drew admiring glances on every hand.

She took his arm. "Tell me something. Why do you fly?"

"It's what I do."

"You're probably filthy rich. Everyone knows the Argentine Air Force is staffed by the aristocracy. You could do anything you want."

"Perhaps I can explain," he said. "When I was a boy, I had an Uncle Juan, my mother's brother, who lived in Mexico City. He was a fabulously wealthy man. A member of one of the oldest families in Mexico and yet, from boyhood, he had room for only one passion."

"Women?"

"No, I'm being serious. Bulls. In fact, he became a *torero,* a professional bullfighter and a great shame to the family because bullfighters are usually gypsies or poor boys, up from the gutter."

"So?"

"I sat with him while they dressed him in his suit of lights for a special appearance at the Grand Plaza in Mexico City. I counted the scars of the horns on his body. Nine times he had been gored. I said, 'Uncle, you have everything. Title, money, power, yet you go to the bulls. You face, week by week, animals specifically trained to kill you. Why do you do this thing?'"

"And what did he reply?"

"He said, 'It's what I am. There's nothing else I want to do.' Flying's like that with me."

She touched the scar. "Even when it almost gets you killed?"

"Ah, but I was younger then. More foolish. I believed in causes, justice, freedom. Beautiful nonsense. Now I am older. All used up."

"We'll have to see about that."

"Is that a promise?"

"Never mind. What happened to your uncle?"

"Oh, he finally went to the horns one time too many."

She shivered. "I don't like it."

41

She had tightened her grip on his arm as if to reassure herself. They crossed from the gardens and started down Kensington Road.

He said, "I think I've done rather well to hold myself in this far, but I feel I must point out that you look spectacularly tarty in that outfit. By intention, I presume?"

"You swine," she said amiably and held his arm even tighter.

"Is one permitted to inquire the purpose?"

She shrugged. "Does it matter? I don't really know. It's nice to play games occasionally, don't you think?"

He stopped, half turned toward her as she still clung to his arm. "You are the most beautiful woman I've ever seen in my life," he said, "in spite of that appalling outfit."

"So kind."

"Think nothing of it. I was wondering if you might be in the market to accept proposals of marriage this morning."

Her whole face went bleak, there was hurt in the green eyes. "Oh, no, Raul, that's not funny. That's not funny at all."

He kissed her gently on the mouth. "Oh, my beautiful, glorious tart. Can't you see how much I'm loving you? I don't have any choice in the business. It's like a moral imperative."

There were tears in her eyes. "Oh, God," she said angrily. "I hate men and yet you're so damn nice. I've never ever known a man quite like you."

He waved to a passing taxi. As it swung in to the

curb she said, "What is this? Where are we going?"

"Back to the flat," he said. "Kensington Palace Gardens. Such a good address. Right next door to the Russian Embassy."

Lying in bed, an arm about her, watching the white curtains rise and fall in the slight breeze from the partly open window, he felt more content, more at peace with himself than he had for years.

There was a radio cassette player on the small table beside the bed. She reached to switch it on and Ella Fitzgerald's unique and wonderful voice moved into "Our Love Is Here to Stay."

"Just for you," she said.

"Very civil of you."

He kissed her lazily on the forehead. She gave a small grunt of infinite content, turned her stomach into his thigh and sighed. "That was lovely. Can we do it again some time?"

"Could you possibly give me time to catch my breath?"

She smiled and ran a hand across his belly. "The poor old man. Just listen to him. Move away a little. I want to look at you."

They lay a couple of feet apart, heads on the same pillow, her green eyes wide and starry as if she was committing him to memory.

"The scar," she said. "Tell me about it."

He shrugged. "I was flying from Fernando Po to Port Harcourt in Biafra during the Nigerian civil war. We usually flew by night. Dakotas mostly, but they needed medical supplies in a hurry." His eyes stared back into the past. "It was raining like hell. A real thunderstorm. I got a Russian MIG fighter on my tail. Egyptian pilot, I found out later. He started to shoot me out of the sky, it was as simple as that. Within seconds the other three crew members were dead or dying. That's when I got this." He fingered the scar.

"What did you do?"

"Took her down to five hundred feet. Next time he came in on my tail, I dropped the Dakota's flaps. It was like stopping dead in mid-air. I almost stalled."

"And the MIG?"

"No space left to work in. Overshot me and plowed straight into the jungle."

"Clever boy."

She ran a finger along his lips. He said drowsily, "I want to be totally honest with you, can you understand that? I've never felt so with any human being before. I want to give all of myself that there is to give."

There was pain in her then because of her deceit. She managed a smile. "Don't worry about it. Go to sleep. We've got all day."

"You're wrong," he said. "We have the rest of our lives." He smiled. "I've always loved cities by night. The marvelous feeling of the potential of things. When I was a young man, walking by night in Paris, London, or Buenos Aires, there was always a magic, something bracing about the night air. A feeling that at the end of the street, something absolutely marvelous was waiting just around the corner."

"What are you trying to tell me?" she asked.

"Forty-five," he said. "Six in July. You've been a long time coming. Thank God you made it. I didn't ask you your sign."

"Capricorn." Her arms were about him now, her lips on his forehead.

"Dreadful combination, Leo and Capricorn," he muttered. "No hope at all."

"Is that a fact?" She kissed him and a moment later he was asleep.

She was standing by the window, looking out across the gardens, thinking about him, when the phone sounded in the sitting room. She went in quickly and picked it up.

Ferguson said, "Ah, there you are. Anything to report?"

"Nothing," she said.

"Is he with you now?"

She took a deep breath. "Yes. Asleep in the other room."

"Things are hotting up," he said. "All the signs point to an invasion down there. You're sure he's staying in London?"

"Yes," she said. "Very sure."

"Fine. I'll be in touch."

She put down the phone, at that moment hating Ferguson more than she had ever hated anyone in her life. There was a sudden sharp cry as Raul Montera called out, and she turned and ran into the bedroom.

The dream was more real than anything he had ever known. The plane was in a hell of a state, he knew that, great holes ripped in the body, pieces of fuselage rattling in the turbulance. He could smell smoke and burning oil. Panic gave him strength as he fought to release the plastic canopy that enveloped him.

"Dear God, don't let me burn," he thought, and then the canopy swung away from him.

His fingers, warm with his own blood, groped for the quick release handle that would eject him, and then a shadow passed overhead. There was a beating of wings and he looked up to find a great eagle, claws distended, dropping down on him, and he screamed aloud in fear. He came awake then, and found himself in Gabrielle's arms.

They sat in the large bath, facing each other, totally at ease, drinking tea from china mugs, Montera smoking a cigarette.

"The tea is excellent," he said.

"Much better for you than coffee," she said.

"From now on, coffee no longer exists."

"An eagle descending," she said. "Quite obviously only one thing to do."

"And what would that be?"

"You told me yourself. Drop your flaps. Even eagles will overshoot."

"Brilliant," he said. "What a pilot you would have made." He stood up and reached for a towel. "What next?"

"I'd like to see *Cats* again."

"But tickets are unobtainable," he said as he started to dress.

"A challenge for you."

"Taken. And dinner afterward?"

"Daphne's, I think. I feel very French today. And make sure they give you a booth."

"At your orders, Señorita," he said formally in Spanish.

As he pulled on his flying jacket, his wallet fell to the floor and among the items that cascaded out there was a small photo. She picked it up and examined it. The woman in the cane chair was beautifully gowned, the hair groomed to perfection, all the arrogance of the true aristocrat in her face. The child who stood beside her wore a formal white dress and was quite tall, with wide dark eyes.

"She's beautiful," Gabrielle said. "A lot like you. But your mother looks as if she could be difficult."

"Donna Elena Llorca de Montera difficult?" He laughed. "Only most of the time."

"Off you go," she said, gathering everything back into his wallet and handing it to him. "I've things to do."

He smiled, moved to the door, and paused. When he turned, he was no longer smiling, but stood there looking extraordinarily vulnerable in the black open-necked shirt and the old flying jacket.

"You really do look gorgeous," she said.

"I've been in the trenches a long time."

"You've got me now," she said in a kind of reflex without thinking.

"Good, then let me do this properly." He dropped to one knee beside the bath. "Do you think there's the remotest possibility that you might be interested in marrying a rather aging fighter pilot who, finding himself too old for jet planes now, may prove rather difficult to handle?"

There were tears in her eyes now and she kissed him, wet from the bath. "Just go! Please just go!"

"Of course." He kissed her gently, then put aside the photo that had fallen on the floor. "You can have that."

The door closed behind him. She stared up at the ceiling, hot, bitter tears washing out of her, thinking of Ferguson, wishing he were dead.

Ferguson was seated at his desk at Cavendish Square with Fox, going through various papers, when the door opened and Villiers pushed in past Kim before the Gurkha could announce him.

"My dear Tony, you look quite agitated," Ferguson said as Kim withdrew.

"What's going on between Gabrielle and this Argentinian, Montera?" Villiers said. "I followed him home last night, so don't attempt to deny it. She's on a job for you, isn't she?"

"None of your business, Tony," Ferguson said. "And neither is she any longer."

Villiers lit a cigarette and paced to the window. "All right, point taken. I can still show concern, can't I? That last job she did for you in Berlin, she nearly ended up in the canal."

"But she didn't," Ferguson said patiently, "because you, dear Tony, turned up in the nick of time as usual. This Montera business is very small beer. She's simply out to extract what useful information she can about the Falklands situation."

"How, by taking him to bed?"

"Not your affair, Tony. And you have, if I may say so, more important things to worry about."

Harry Fox passed a note across. "They've canceled your leave, Tony. They want you back in Hereford as soon as possible."

Bradbury Lines, Hereford, was the headquarters of the 22nd Special Air Service Regiment.

"But why, for God's sake?" Villiers demanded.

Ferguson sighed and removed his reading glasses. "Quite simple really, Tony. I think you may be going to war sooner than you think."

And at his flat off Belgrave Square, Raul Montera gripped the telephone tightly, listening with horror to what the air and military attaché at the Embassy was saying to him.

"There is a plane for Paris leaving in two hours, Raul. It is essential that you do not miss it. The Air France flight for Buenos Aires leaves at ten-thirty this evening. They need you back there, my friend. You mustn't fail. I'm sending a car around now."

The Malvinas. That's all it could be. So many things fell into place now. Yet there was Gabrielle. What was he going to do about her? My one real chance of happiness in this accursed life, he thought, and the lesser gods decide to screw it up for me.

He packed hurriedly, just one bag with essentials, and the doorbell rang as he was finishing. The chauffeur was waiting on the step as Montera emerged still wearing his jeans and the old flying jacket.

"Heathrow, my colonel," the chauffeur said as Montera got into the front seat beside him.

"By way of Kensington Palace Gardens," Raul Montera said. "And step on it! We don't have much time."

Gabrielle had not changed, was sitting at the mirror in the old robe and about to make herself up, when the doorbell buzzed. She went and lifted the intercom.

"It's me, Raul. Please hurry."

She half opened the door and waited, conscious of a dreadful foreboding, heard the elevator door clang outside. He appeared, eyes wild, real pain on his face.

"Two minutes, that's all I've got. I've got a plane to catch to Paris. I've been recalled to Buenos Aires."

"But why?" she cried.

"Does it matter?" He took her by the arms and kissed her savagely, all his anger and frustration pouring out of him. "All I've got time for. Isn't life hell?"

He turned and was gone. The elevator door clanged

again. She stood there, frozen, then ran into the bedroom and started to dress.

At Heathrow, Montera was just about to go through into the international departure lounge when she called his name, high and clear. As he turned, she came running through the crowd in a yellow cotton jumpsuit, hair tousled, face pale.

She ran into his arms. He held her for a moment, then pushed her away. "You look wonderful."

"Nonsense," she said. "My hair's a mess, no make-up, and wearing the first thing that came to hand."

"Wonderful," he said. "Did I find time to tell you that I've now discovered what joy is? Thank you for that."

"Raul, I love you. I love you so much."

He smiled. "We have a saying. Love is a gift that must be returned fourfold. What a burden you place on me. What a wonderful burden."

Above their heads the loudspeaker called his name.

"Will you write?" she demanded.

"It may be difficult. Don't worry, even if there is a gap for a while. There are good reasons. I'll be back, I swear it. That's all that matters."

She moved with him to the gate, hanging on. He turned for the last time. "I'll make a bargain with you. No more partings ever again. No more saying goodbye. This is the last time. The only time."

And then he was gone, and she turned her face into a pillar and wept. After a while, she crossed to the telephones and dialed Ferguson's number, reversing the charge.

"He's gone," she said. "Just left for Paris to make a connection for Buenos Aires."

"Rather sudden," Ferguson said. "Did he explain?"

"No."

"You sound upset, Gabrielle."

She told him what to do then, in French of the kind definitely not taught in any finishing school—sharp, succinct, and to the point—slammed down the receiver and walked away.

When she opened the door of the flat and went in, Villiers appeared from the bedroom.

"Sorry about this," he said. "My leave's been canceled and they want me back at Hereford. I needed a few things."

He went back into the bedroom and returned to packing the bag that was open on the bed. She followed him through, her rage and frustration focusing on him.

"A few more throats need cutting somewhere, is that it?"

"I suppose so."

"How was Belfast this time?"

"Pretty awful."

"Good—you deserve each other."

He closed the case and said calmly, "I used to think that had a special significance where we were concerned."

"No, Tony," she said. "Whatever else I may have deserved in this life, I didn't deserve you."

"What did I do?" he said. "What terrible thing did I do that you should hate me so, because you do, you know."

"I married a stranger," she said. "Oh, you looked wonderful in uniform, Tony, and then it started. Every rotten little war that came along, you had to volunteer. Borneo, the Oman, Ireland. Even Vietnam, for Christ's sake. God, what I could say about that and you and your precious SAS if it wasn't for the Official Secrets Act."

His face was bleak. "This isn't getting us anywhere."

"You're good at one thing, Tony. One thing only are you truly good at. Killing people."

He pointed at the bed, the pillows still crumpled from where she had lain with Raul Montera, and picked up the white skirt and yellow T-shirt that still lay on the floor where she had dropped them.

"I've heard of in the line of duty, Gabrielle, but this does really seem to be taking it too far."

Her face crumpled as she slumped down on the bed. "I love him so much, Tony. I never knew love could be like this and he's gone. He's gone."

Villiers picked up his bag and stood there, a wave of jealousy and helplessness washing over him. Conscious of the desolation in her voice, he tried to speak, but there was really nothing he could say. He turned and went out, slowly closing the door behind him.

* * *

Ferguson, still at his desk, stretched himself wearily. Paper and yet more paper. It never seemed to stop. He got up and, going to the window, peered out into the square. Behind him, the door from the office opened and Harry Fox rushed in.

"Signal just in, sir. Units of the Argentine fleet have detached themselves from maneuvers and are proceeding toward the Falkland Islands." He handed the signal sheet to Ferguson. "What do you think it means, sir?"

"Well, I never thought to have to say this again in my lifetime. Harry, but believe it or not, I think it means war."

5

A cold wind lifted across the Seine and dashed rain against the windows of the all-night café by the bridge. It was a poor sort of place, usually much frequented by prostitutes, but not on such a night, or rather, morning, for it was almost 5:00 A.M.

The barman leaned on the zinc-topped counter reading a newspaper, and Nikolai Belov sat at a table in the corner drinking coffee, the only customer.

Belov was in his early fifties, and for twelve years had been cultural attaché at the Soviet Embassy in Paris. His dark suit was of English cut, as was the dark blue overcoat that fitted him to perfection. He was a handsome, rather fleshy man with a mane of silver hair, which made him look more like a distinguished actor than what he was, a colonel in the KGB.

The coffee was really rather good and he said to the barman, "I'll have another and a cognac. Is that the early edition you have there?"

The barman nodded. "Hot off the press at four o'clock. Have a look if you like. The news is all bad for the British down there in the Falklands."

Belov sipped his cognac and read the front page. Argentine Skyhawks had continued to bomb the British task force at San Carlos and Falkland Sound.

"Monsieur, this Exocet missile is formidable," the barman said. "What a weapon, and all French. You fire it from forty miles away, it drops to the surface and skims the waves at ten feet, just under the speed of sound. There was an article about it in *Paris Match* yesterday. The damn thing can't miss."

Which wasn't quite true, but Belov wasn't prepared to argue. "A triumph for French technology." He raised his glass and the barman toasted him back.

The door opened in a flurry of wind and rain and a man entered. He was small, dark haired, with thin features and a mustache. His raincoat was quite wet and he carried an umbrella that he was experiencing difficulty in closing. His name was Juan Garcia and he was a First Secretary in the Commercial Department of the Argentine Embassy in Paris. In reality, he was a major in military intelligence.

"Nikolai." He spoke in good French and held out his hand with genuine warmth. "It's good to see you."

"And you," Belov said. "Try the coffee. It's really excellent, and the cognac will certainly clear your pipes."

He nodded to the barman and lit a cigarette, waiting for Garcia to take off his wet coat. The barman brought the coffee and cognac and departed to the kitchen in back.

"You said it was urgent," Belov said. "I certainly hope so. This is an appalling time in the morning to be about."

"It is urgent," Garcia said. "Of the utmost importance to my country. You've seen the morning paper?"

"Indeed I have. You seem to be giving our British friends a hard time. Another frigate blown up, a destroyer damaged. The toll is mounting."

"Unfortunately there is another side to all this," Garcia said. "So far, around half our Skyhawk fighter bombers are not making it back to base. A quite unacceptable loss rate."

"To put it frankly, you'll be running out of pilots before you know where you are. On the other hand, the British fleet does have to sit it out as best it can in Falkland Sound and San Carlos Water and you still have the Exocet. The attack on the *Sheffield* speaks for itself."

"But we don't have enough," Garcia said. "Two were launched against *Sheffield*, one missed altogether. There have been other attacks where they've been launched unsuccessfully. It takes time to get used to such a weapon. We think we've worked it out now. We've had the right kind of assistance."

"From French experts?"

"President Mitterand would deny it, but yes, we have had French help with the missile launchers and control systems. And we have, of course, a squadron of Super Étendard bombers, which are absolutely essential to the whole task. I'm no technician but apparently their radar system is compatible with the Exocet, which can't be used with a Mirage, for example."

There was something he was holding back. Belov said gently, "Better tell me, Juan."

Garcia stirred his coffee, obviously under considerable stress. "A few days ago a unit of the British Special Air Service made a commando attack on our air base at Rio Gallegos. They managed to destroy six Super Étendards."

Belov, who had known of the incident in finest detail for some days, nodded sympathetically. "That must really reduce your capability."

"Of course, we have dispersed the other Étendards to secret locations. And we still have enough to do the job."

"Which is?"

"The British have two aircraft carriers, *Hermes* and *Invincible*. Sink either one and the effect on their air cover would be dramatic. They would be forced to withdraw the fleet."

"And you think this can be done?"

"Our experts say only a question of time, but we need more Exocets." He hammered his fist on the table.

"Which the French, under pressure from the European Community, won't give you."

"Exactly."

"I heard the Libyans were going to help."

"You know what Qaddafi is like. A hell of a lot of talk. Oh, he might do something eventually, but by then it will be too late."

There was silence. Belov lit an American cigarette. "So what do you want from me, my friend?" he asked gently.

"Your government has helped us already. Discreetly, it is true. Satellite information and so on, but all very useful. We know you're on our side in this."

"No, Juan," Belov said. "On this one, we don't take sides."

Garcia was exasperated and showed it. "For God's sake, you want to see the British defeated, don't pretend. It will suit your purposes very well and the psychological effect of such a defeat on the Atlantic Alliance would be disastrous."

"So what do you want?"

"Exocets. I have the money to pay. Ample funds in Geneva in gold or any currency you like. All I want from you is the name, a contact. Don't tell me you can't do something."

Nikolai Belov sat there looking at him for a moment, then glanced at his watch. "All right, leave it with me. I'll be in touch later this morning. Not at the Embassy. Be at your flat."

"You mean you've got somebody?"

"Perhaps. Go now. I'll follow later."

Garcia departed. The door closed behind him. A small wind drifted around the room, lifting a paper on the floor in the corner. Belov shivered, looking around him at the squalor with distaste, and stood up.

The barman came in from the kitchen. "Anything else, Monsieur?"

"I don't think so." Belov dropped a note on the counter and buttoned his coat. "I wonder if God really knew what he was doing when he made mornings like this?"

He opened the door and departed.

Belov lived in an apartment on the top floor of a luxury building of some distinction on the boulevard St. Germain. He went straight there from his assignation with Garcia. He was tired and cold, and the prospect of Irana Vronsky waiting for him filled him with conscious pleasure. She was a handsome, full-bodied woman of thirty-five and undeniably attractive. She had been Belov's secretary for ten years or more, and he had seduced her within a month of her taking up the appointment. She was totally devoted to him.

When she opened the door to him, she was wearing a superb black silk dressing gown, which gaped as she moved forward, revealing black stockings and the hint of a garter belt.

Belov took her in his arms. "You smell wonderful."

There was concern on her face. "Nikolai, you're frozen. Let me get you some coffee. What was it all about?"

"First the coffee," he said. "We go to bed and you warm me up. Then I tell you what Garcia wanted and you can put that fine common sense of yours to work."

Later, lying sideways in bed, watching him smoke a cigarette, she said, "Why bother, Nikolai? They're a bunch of fascists down there in Argentina. Under military rule, thousands have disappeared. I'd rather have the British any day of the week."

"Keep that up, you'll have me defecting, just so you can live in Kensington and shop at Harrods every day." He smiled and then became serious. "There is more than one reason for taking an interest in this business. A mini-war we are not involved in personally is always useful when it has two anti-Communist countries at each other's throats. A great deal of technical information can be derived from their use of weaponry and so on."

"Good point."

"An even better one is this, Irana. Exocets or no Exocets, the British are going to win this war. Oh, the Argentine Air Force has performed magnificently, but their Navy stays in harbor and their army of occupation in the Falklands consists mainly of conscripts. I shudder to think what British marines and paratroopers will do to them once they start rolling."

"What are you saying then? That you won't help Garcia?"

"Not at all. I'm all in favor of giving him exactly what he wants, but what if one could do it in such a way that it would entirely discredit the ruling junta in Argentina? If we could only bring down the military government, Irana, the opportunities of government by the people would be limitless."

"My God," she said. "What an imagination. You already see a Russian fleet installed in Rio Gallegos, controlling the South Atlantic."

"I know; beautiful, isn't it?"

He lay there for a while longer and she ran the fingers of her right hand up over his thigh and across his belly. He grabbed her hand and pushed it away, a sudden excitement on his face.

"I have it. Donner. This should suit him down to the ground. Where is he?"

"In London this week, I think."

"Get him on the phone now. Tell him to get the shuttle from Heathrow. I want to see him here before noon."

She got out of bed and went to the phone as Belov lit another cigarette, thoroughly pleased with himself.

Felix Donner was a magnificent figure of a man, at least six foot three with a great breadth of shoulder and dark hair swept back from his forehead. As chairman of the Donner Development Corporation, he was a well-known and highly respected figure in London financial circles.

Everyone knew his story. The Australian from Rum Jungle, south of Darwin in the Northern Territory, who had served with the Australian Army in Korea where he had been a prisoner of the Chinese for two years. He had then come to London where he'd hacked his way up to his first million in the property boom of the sixties. Since then he'd never looked back. His interests were varied—from shipping to electronics.

He was a popular figure with the media and was often photographed mingling with the stars at a film première, playing polo, shooting grouse, even shaking hands with royalty at a charity dinner.

It was rather ironic when one considered that this benign and popular man was in reality one Victor Marchuk, a Ukrainian who had not seen his homeland for thirty years now.

The Russians had a number of spy schools at various places in the Soviet Union, each one with a distinctive national flavor, like Glacyna where agents were trained to work in English-speaking countries in a replica of an English town, living exactly as they did in the West.

The original Felix Donner, an orphan with no relatives, had been specially selected from a Chinese prison camp and transported to Glacyna where Marchuk could observe him as closely as any prize specimen in a laboratory. And it was Marchuk who was eventually returned to Chinese custody to labor in a Manchurian coal mine. As by arrangement he was the only one of the six members of his original unit captured to survive, there was no one to identify the gaunt scarecrow of a man about twenty-five pounds underweight, who was released the following year.

But he looked healthy enough as he stood up and stretched later that morning, just before noon, and went to the window of Belov's apartment.

"Interesting possibilities."

"You think you might be able to do something?" Belov asked.

Donner shrugged. "I don't know. Let's have a talk with this Argentinian, Garcia. Tell him to come round with everything he's got on this whole Exocet thing. Then we see."

"Good," Belov said. "I knew I could rely on you. Excuse me. I'll phone him from my study."

He went out, and Irana Vronsky came in with fresh coffee. Her hair was tied back with a black bow, and her neat gray skirt, white blouse, dark stockings, only accentuated her undeniable charms.

Donner slid his arms around her waist and pulled her against him, savoring her.

"Is Nikolai looking after you all right?" he said in Russian. "If not, just let me know. Always glad to help."

"Bastard," she said.

"It's been said before," he laughed as she left the room.

Juan Garcia sat by the window with Nikolai Belov and drank coffee in silence, while on the other side of the room Felix Donner sat in a wingback chair by the fire and worked his way through the bulky file the Argentinian had provided.

After a while, the Australian closed the file and

reached for a cigarette. "An extraordinary business. The Étendard is manufactured by Dassault, in which the French government has a 51 percent holding."

"That's correct," Garcia said.

"And the makers of the Exocet are the state-owned Aérospatiale Industries, the president of which is General Jacques Mitterand, brother of the President of France? An intriguing situation in view of the fact that the French Government has suspended all military aid to Argentina."

Garcia said, "On the other hand, we were lucky enough to have a team of French technicians already in my country before the outbreak of hostilities. Based at Bahia Blanca, they have given invaluable assistance as regards testing and fitting the missile launchers and control systems."

"And you have also had other help, I see from the file. This man Bernard, Dr. Paul Bernard, would seem to have supplied you with information crucial to the success of the operation."

"A brilliant electronic engineer," Garcia said. "At one time head of one of the research sections at Aérospatiale. Now a professor at the Sorbonne."

"His motives interest me," Donner said. "What are they exactly? Money?"

"No, it seems he has no love for the English. He phoned the Embassy at the start of things, when President Mitterand announced the embargo. He offered to help in any way he could."

"Interesting," Donner said.

"We have considerable sympathy here in many

quarters," Garcia added. "Traditionally, France and Britain have never enjoyed what could be termed a warm relationship."

Donner opened the file and looked at it again, frowning. Belov waited, admiring the performance.

Garcia said, "Can you help us?"

"I think so. I can say no more than that at this stage. On a purely business footing, of course. Frankly, I'm not interested in the rights and wrongs of this affair. If I can work something out, find you a few Exocets, I should imagine it would cost you in the region of two to three million."

"Dollars?" Garcia asked.

"My operations are based in the City of London, Señor Garcia," Donner told him. "I only deal in pounds sterling. And in gold. Do you have that much available?"

Garcia swallowed hard. "No problem. The necessary funds are in Geneva now."

"Good." Donner stood up. "I should like to speak to Professor Bernard."

"When?" Garcia asked.

"As soon as possible." Donner looked at his watch. "Let's say at two this afternoon. Somewhere nice and open."

"Two o'clock?" Garcia looked hunted. "I don't know. It's very short notice. It may not be convenient."

"Then I suggest you make it convenient," Donner told him. "After all, time is of the essence in this affair. If we are to do anything, it must be within a week, or ten days at the outside. After that, I should have thought it would be too late. Wouldn't you agree?"

"Of course," Garcia said hurriedly and turned to Belov. "May I use the phone?"

"In the study."

Garcia went out. Belov said, "You have an idea, I think?"

"Possibly," Donner said. "Something in that file that could suit our purposes admirably."

"You'll be staying in your apartment in the rue de Rivoli, I suppose?"

"That's right. Wanda has gone ahead to make sure everything's in apple-pie order.

"How is she? As beautiful as ever?"

"Did I ever settle for anything less?"

Belov laughed. "I wonder what you'd do if they decided to recall you home to Moscow after all these years?"

"Home?" Donner said. "Where's that? And they wouldn"t. I'm too valuable where I am. I'm the best there is, you know that."

Belov shook his head. "I don't understand you, Felix. Why do you do it? You're certainly no patriot, and politics you find games for children — you've told me that often enough."

"It's the only game in town," Donner said. "I enjoy every minute of it. I like beating them, Nikolai, whoever *they* are."

Belov nodded. "I believe you. I really do. Is Stavrou with you?"

"Downstairs in the car."

The study door opened and Garcia entered. "Fine,' he said. "All organized."

The meeting with Bernard took place on a tourist barge on the Seine, although because of the heavy rain there were few tourists in evidence. Donner and Bernard sat under an awning at a table in the stern, a bottle of Sancerre between them. At the rail a few yards away, leaned a man who was even taller than Donner, watching the passing scenery. He wore a raincoat over a dark blue suit, black tie, and white shirt. His gray hair was cropped to the skull and he had a flat-boned face whose slanted eyes and open nostrils gave him a faintly Mongolian appearance.

This was Yanni Stavrou, half Turkish, the other half anyone's guess. A French national because of service in Algiers as a French Foreign Legion paratrooper, he was a supremely dangerous man. Donner's chauffeur, bodyguard, and strong right arm for ten years now.

Professor Bernard said, "I thought Garcia would be here?"

"Not necessary," Donner said. "I've heard everything there is to be heard from him. They need more Exocets desperately."

"I can imagine. What is your interest in this affair?"

"They've asked me to find them some. You've already helped them considerably, to a degree extremely dangerous for a man in your position if it became known. Why did you take such a risk?"

"Because I didn't think the arms embargo was right. The government was wrong. We shouldn't have taken sides."

"But you have. Why?"

Bernard shrugged. "I don't like the English."

"Not good enough."

"Not good enough?" Bernard's voice rose angrily so that Stavrou turned from the rail, watchful. "Let me tell you about the English. In 1940, they ran. Left us to the Germans. When the Boche came to our village, my father and a few others tried to put up a fight. A handful of farmers with World War One rifles. They shot them in the square. My mother and most of the other women they took into the village hall to make sport for the soldiers. I was ten years old. A long time ago, but I can still hear the screaming." He spat over the side. "So don't try to tell me about the English."

Donner couldn't have been more delighted. "Terrible," he said. "I understand perfectly."

"But you," Bernard said. "You are English yourself. I don't understand."

"Australian," Donner said. "A large difference. Also a citizen of the world and a businessman, so let's get down to business. Tell me about Île de Roc."

"Île de Roc?" Bernard looked bewildered.

"They're testing the latest Exocet there, aren't they? You told Garcia about that. It's in your notes."

"Yes, of course. It's an island. A damn great rock really, about fifteen miles off the Brittany coast, south from St. Nazaire. If you look out to sea, all there is is the Atlantic and then Newfoundland."

"How many people there?"

"No more than thirty-five. A mixture of Aéro-spatiale technicians and army personnel from missile regiments. In fact, it's officially a military installation."

"You've been there?"

"Certainly. On a number of occasions."

"And how does one get to the island, by air?"

"Oh, no, impossible. Nowhere to land. Well, that's not quite true. The Army Air Corps managed to land light aircraft on one of the beaches when the tide was out, but it wasn't a practical proposition. Even helicopters find it difficult because of the downdrafts from the cliffs. The weather is frequently terrible, but of course the isolation of the place was a necessary factor. Usually, the link with the mainland is by boat. The fishing port of St. Martin."

Donner nodded. "Say I needed to know what was going on at Île de Roc, let's say during the next week or ten days. Could you find out? Are your contacts still good?"

"Excellent," Bernard said. "I think I can guarantee to obtain any information you require and at the shortest of notice."

Donner refilled his glass. "This Sancerre is really very fine." He looked at Stavrou. "I think we'll have another bottle." He lit a cigarette, leaned back in his chair, and said to Bernard, "Okay, fill me in on the island. For example, tell me in detail about your last trip there."

Wanda Jones was a graceful woman, the soft contours of whose body were accentuated by the white silk blouse and black velvet skirt she wore, but she was still small in spite of the high-heeled shoes. Her hair was black as night, she had wide, almond-shaped eyes and a small, corrupt mouth. Her appearance was one of extreme elegance, for she had learned the hard way, Donner's cardinal rule, that less is always better.

She was one-quarter Negro, which showed in her skin, and when she opened her mouth her London East End origin was plain.

Donner had picked her, quite literally, off a Soho street one night where her current boyfriend had been attempting rather forcibly to introduce her into a life of prostitution. Stavrou had left him in a doorway with two ribs and his left arm broken, and Wanda had found herself plunged headlong into a world of luxury and delight.

She had been all of sixteen, but then Donner had always had an eye for attractive women, no matter what age. Her one fear was that he might discard her for someone he found more appealing.

When she went into his study in the sumptuous apartment in the Rue de Rivoli, he turned in the swivel chair behind the desk. His arms were folded, and he was looking at a large-scale map he'd had

Stavrou procure that afternoon of Île de Roc and the coastal area around St. Martin. He had already discussed the problem with her in bed after making love to her that afternoon. He had never kept secrets from her, and she clung to the belief that it was evidence of trust.

She put down the coffee she had brought him and put an arm around his neck. He slipped a hand under her skirt in an absent-minded way and stroked her thigh.

"You think there's a way?" she asked.

"Oh, yes, there's always a way, if one looks close enough."

"Nikolai and this man Garcia are here."

"Good." He turned and kissed her neck, pulling her on to his knee. "I've told Stavrou to hire a private plane. I want you to fly down here," he pointed at the map, "to this St. Martin place first thing in the morning. See if you can find us a house in the area. Something substantial that's immediately available. There's bound to be something. Always is in that kind of country area."

"Anything else?"

"Maybe later. Now show Nikolai and Garcia in."

She went out and a moment later the two men entered. Donner got up and walked to the window, stretching. The view of the city was panoramic and always delighted him.

"Thank God it's stopped raining."

Garcia said impatiently. "Please, Señor Donner. You said you would have news for me."

Donner turned. "But I do. It's all in hand, my friend. In fact I think I can guarantee you, let's say, ten of the latest mark of Exocet missiles by next Monday."

Garcia gazed at him in awe. "Can this be so, Señor?"

"Definitely. You can leave it all in my hands. Just one thing for you to do. I want an Argentine Air Force officer to liaise with me on this one. No desk type either. Preferably a first-rate pilot. After all, it's only a fifteen-hour flight from Buenos Aires to Paris. You get a message off tonight, and he could be here tomorrow or the next day."

"Of course, Señor. I'll get a message off right away. And the financial arrangements?"

"We'll settle all that later."

Garcia left and Donner went to the liquor cabinet and poured whisky into two glasses.

"What are you up to?" Belov demanded.

Donner handed him one of the glasses. "How would it suit you if, in getting these Exocets, I dropped the Argentinians right in the manure, the French breaking off diplomatic relations, a real international scandal? How would you like that?"

"I think I'd like it immensely," Belov said. "Tell me more."

So Donner did, in finest detail.

6

Ferguson worked late that evening at his office. The Directorate-General of the Security Service for Group Four more than had its hands full these days. In addition to bringing its normal antiterrorist role into play against the possibility of Argentine undercover units infiltrating London, Ferguson had been given responsibility by the Director-General himself for handling and coordinating all operations connected with Exocet.

Harry Fox came in looking tired, shirtsleeves rolled up to the elbow. "I've just had the good word in from Peru. Our people there, in cooperation with anti-government guerrillas, destroyed a military convoy earlier today that was carrying five Exocets to a Peruvian Air Force base near Lima for onward transportation to Argentina."

"Thank God for that. What about the Libyans?"

"Qaddafi seems to be having second thoughts. Both

King Hussein and the Egyptian government have asked him to keep out of it."

"Which really only leaves the manufacturers, Harry. All right, we know there's been a certain amount of French technical assistance, but that, after all, has been mainly a product of circumstance. The men involved were already there."

"An interesting question, sir. What would we do if we had trouble with our own Exocet missiles? Expect the French to render technical assistance?"

"We don't wish to know that, Harry. Get back to work."

Rain dashed against the window pane. He peered out and shivered, thinking of the fleet down there in the South Atlantic and winter rolling in.

"God help sailors at sea on a night like this," he said softly.

It was very quiet in the small study in the Residencia del Presidente at Olivos outside Buenos Aires. The President himself, General Leopoldo Fortunato Galtieri, was in uniform, but had taken off his tunic as he sat at the desk working his way through a mass of papers.

He was a bull of a man, plain spoken, a soldier's soldier. He had frequently been compared to that most colorful of all American generals of World War Two, George S. Patton.

There was a knock at the door, and a young army captain in dress uniform looked in.

The President glanced up. "What is it, Martinez?"

"General Dozo is here, sir."

"Good, show him in. See that we are not disturbed. No phone calls for half an hour." He smiled, suddenly looking relaxed and charming. "Of course, if news comes in that either the *Hermes* or *Invincible* has been sunk, disturb me all you like."

"At your orders, my President."

Martinez withdrew, and a moment later Brigadier General Basilio Lami Dozo, commander of the Argentine Air Force, entered. An elegant, handsome man whose uniform fitted him to perfection, a natural aristocrat, in total contrast to Galtieri who had been born into a working-class family and had come up the hard way.

They, with the commander of the Navy, Admiral Jorge Anaya, worked together as the three-man junta that ruled the country.

Lami Dozo took off his cap and lit a cigarette. "Isn't Anaya coming?"

Galtieri was pouring cognac into two glasses at the drinks cabinet. "What for? We might as well not have a Navy for all the good it does. Thank God for the Air Force. True heroes, all those lads of yours." He handed Lami Dozo a glass. "Here's to them."

"What's left of them," Lami Dozo said bitterly and drank a little cognac. "Things are so bad down there at Gallegos that everyone who can fly is going up. Raul Montera, for God's sake. Forty-six next birthday and he's flying Skyhawks to San Carlos Water." He shook his head. "I sometimes think I should be back in a cockpit myself."

"Don't be ridiculous," Galtieri said. "Raul Montera always was a romantic fool."

"And a true hero."

"Oh, I'll give you that. Magnificent. I have every admiration for him."

"That's what the boys call him. El Magnifico. He can't last, of course. He's flown eleven operations during the past week to my knowledge." He shook his head. "God knows what I'll find to say to his mother when he goes."

"Donna Elena?" Galtieri shuddered. "Keep her away from me, whatever you do. That woman always makes me feel I should be herding cows, barefooted. How was it today?"

"We hit a frigate, HMS *Antelope*. When I last heard, there had been some sort of explosion and she was on fire. We think we also damaged a destroyer, the *Glasgow*, but we can't be sure. Six Mirages and two Skyhawks were shot down. Some made it back to base damaged." He shook his head in wonder. "And in spite of that, the spirit of those boys is fantastic. But it can't go on. We'll run out of pilots."

"Exactly," Galtieri said. "Which is why we need more Exocets, and according to this report just in from our Embassy in Paris, we could have exactly what we need in a matter of days. Read it."

He went to the window and looked out at the gardens, bright in the sunshine, as he finished his cognac. Behind him, Lami Dozo said, "You could be right. But Garcia doesn't seem to have any information as to how or where this man Donner intends to obtain Exocets."

"True, but he is convinced that Donner can supply and it's worth a try. You notice, of course, that they ask for a top Air Force officer to liaise on this one, preferably a pilot."

"Yes."

"Does anyone spring to mind as being particularly suitable for the job?" He turned inquiringly.

Lami Dozo smiled. "It would keep him alive, wouldn't it, and as a matter of coincidence, he does speak excellent French."

"No time to lose. He should be on his way to Paris tomorrow."

Lami Dozo picked up his cap. "No problem. I'll fly down to Gallegos myself in the Lear Jet. Bring him back with me."

"Good, I'd like a word before he goes." As Lami Dozo moved toward the door, Galtieri called, "You know what the day after tomorrow is?"

"Of course." It was Tuesday, May 25, and Argentina's national day.

"You've something special planned, I trust?"

"We'll do our best."

Lami Dozo went out. The President sighed, sat down at his desk, and resumed work.

In London, Gabrielle Legrand, shopping in Harrods, found herself walking through the television department. A small crowd had gathered before a large television set and the ITV news was on. The screen was showing a still picture of San Carlos Water, ships scattered at action in a cloud of smoke. As another picture flashed on the screen an anonymous voice was describing a flight of Argentine Skyhawks cutting across the water, every gun in the fleet blazing at them.

His voice lifted in excitement as he followed the track of a Rapier missile. There was a sound of an explosion and another view of what was left of the Skyhawk dropping into the sea.

Several people in the crowd applauded, and a man said, "Got the bastard."

It was so understandable. This was the enemy they were looking at, planes dedicated to destroying their own boys. One of those boys was her half brother, Richard. She knew he was on one of the aircraft carriers two hundred miles to the west of San Carlos Water, but that was not safety. Helicopter pilots like Richard flew toward danger every day, and the carriers were the constant targets of the Argentine missiles. Gabrielle prayed that God would protect twenty-two-year-olds.

Another fighter plane picture flashed across the television screen, and she turned away, feeling sick.

Thank God Raul's too old to fly those things, she thought, and hurried out.

Raul Montera, at that actual moment, was in an Argentinian fighter plane, fifty miles off the southern tip of Argentina, five hundred feet above the sea. Another Skyhawk was in the air two hundred yards to the northwest of him. Most of its tail was missing, and a plume of smoke drifted gently behind it. He was trying to nurse it home.

The boy in the cockpit was badly wounded, and Montera had long since abandoned any attempt at proper procedure.

"Hang on, José, not long now."

"No use, Colonel." The boy's voice was very tired. "She's going down. I can't hold her any longer."

As the Skyhawk's nose dipped, Montera said, "Eject, boy."

"And freeze to death?" the boy laughed faintly. "Why bother."

"Lieutenant Ortega," Montera cried. "Eject now. That's an order."

A second later, the canopy flew into space, the boy was catapulted out. Montera followed him down, already giving base the position, watching the parachute drift, hoping that the air-sea rescue launch would be in time.

He made a quick pass as Ortega hit the water, saw him break free of the chute. The small yellow dinghy inflated, and as he watched, the boy tried to climb in.

There was a sudden warning buzz from the instrument panel that told him how low he was on fuel. He made one more pass, waggled his wings, and curled away toward the coast.

* * *

When Montera got out of the cockpit of the Skyhawk at the Gallegos base, Sergeant Santerra, the technical crew chief, was already examining the plane and shaking his head.

"Look at the tail, for Christ's sake, Colonel. Cannon shell, at least four. Holes all over the place."

"I know. We had a couple of Harriers on our tails on the way out of San Carlos. They got Santini. Young Ortega almost made it and ditched about fifty miles out."

"Your luck is good, Colonel. Amazing. I can't understand it. You should have been dead days ago."

"I put it all down to the love of a good woman, myself." Raul Montera reached up and touched the name "Gabrielle," which was painted on the side of the cockpit. "Thank you, my love."

When he went into the Intelligence Room in the operations building, it was empty except for Major Pedro Munro, an Argentinian of Scots extraction, the senior intelligence officer.

"Ah, there you are, Raul. One of these days you won't walk through that door," he said cheerfully.

"Thanks very much," Montera told him. "Any word on Ortega?"

"Not yet. What have you got to tell me?"

Montera helped himself to a cigarette from the pack on the desk. "That it was hell out there, just like an old war movie on television, only this was real. Men died."

Munro said, "Very funny. Now, could I possibly have something concrete? Did you sink anything?"

"I don't think so," Montera told him, "for the excellent reason that my bombs didn't explode again. Could you possibly arrange for ordnance to get the blasted timing right on those fuses?"

And Munro stopped trying to be amusing. "I'm damn sorry, Raul. Truly."

"So am I," Montera told him and went out.

He walked toward the officers' mess wearily, his flying boots drumming on the pavement. He felt totally depressed, stale, at the final end of things. He was too old to be doing this sort of thing, that was a fact, and then he remembered what Gabrielle had said to him about age being a state of mind and smiled.

He thought a lot about her these days. In fact, all the time. She filled his heart and head, flew with him, slept with him. He spoke aloud to her last thing each night. It was really quite incredible.

He walked into the anteroom and the first person he saw was Lami Dozo standing by the fire, a circle of young officers about him.

The general excused himself and came to meet Montera, genuine pleasure on his face. He gave him the *abrazo*, the formal hug.

"I saw your mother yesterday at a charity affair. Fund raising for the Army."

"Was Linda with her?"

"No, she was at school. Your mother looked splendid. You, on the other hand, look perfectly dreadful.

It must stop, this foolishness, Raul Eleven missions in a week."

"Twelve," Montera said. "You forget today, and could you kindly get them to do something about the bombs? They will persist in not going off a lot of the time. Very annoying when one has gone to such a great deal of trouble to deliver them."

"Have a drink," Lami Dozo said.

"An excellent idea." Montera called a mess waiter over. 'Tea. My usual." He turned to the general. "Will you join me?"

"Tea?" Lami Dozo said. "Good God, what's got into you?"

Montera nodded to the waiter, who departed. "Nothing. It's just that a friend of mine, when I was in London, persuaded me that coffee wasn't good for me."

"Who is this Gabrielle whose name they tell me is painted on the nose of your Skyhawk?"

"The woman I love," Raul Montera said simply.

"Have I had the pleasure of meeting her."

"No. When she isn't living in London, she lives in Paris. Next question."

"Paris? How interesting. If you have time, you could look her up."

"I don't understand?"

"You're flying to Paris tomorrow. I'm taking you back to Buenos Aires with me now. Oh, and Galtieri would like a word before you leave."

"I think perhaps you'd better explain," Montera said.

Which Lami Dozo did as briefly as possible. When he was finished he said, "Well, what do you think?"

"I think the world has gone mad," Raul Montera told him. "But who am I to argue."

"It could win us the war, Raul."

"Win us the war?" Montera laughed harshly. "We're back with old movies on television, General. We've lost this war already. It should never have started, but by all means send me off to Paris to play games while these boys here continue to die."

The waiter returned with the tray at that moment and Montera poured himself a cup of tea with hands that shook slightly.

He raised the cup to his lips and drank. "Much better for you than coffee," he said and smiled, remembering that morning in Kensington, a thousand years ago, in the bath with Gabrielle.

Lami Dozo looked concerned. "You've done too much, old friend. You need a rest. Come on, let's go."

"You think I'm going over the edge." Montera swallowed the rest of his tea. "You're quite wrong. I'm already there."

As they stood up, Major Munro came in. He glanced about the mess, saw Montera, and smiled. "Good news, Raul. Young Ortega—they've picked him up. Badly shot up, but he'll survive. They say it was the coldness of the sea that saved him. Stopped him bleeding to death."

He recognized the general in the same moment and saluted.

"His luck is good," Lami Dozo commented.

"Let's hope mine is," said Raul Montera.

A little under four hours later, he was following Lami Dozo into Galtieri's private study at the Residencia del Presidente.

Galtieri came around the desk to greet him warmly, hand outstretched. "My dear Montera, a great pleasure. Your efforts on behalf of the cause have been heroic."

"I've done no more than any other pilot in my command, General."

"Very commendable, but not quite true. However, General Dozo has briefed you, I'm sure, on the importance of this new mission. We're all counting on you."

"I'll do my best, General. May I have permission to visit my mother before I leave?"

"But of course. Give Donna Elena my humble duty. And now, I'll detain you no longer."

He shook hands again and Montera and Lami Dozo departed. When they had gone, Galtieri flicked the intercom and told Martinez to come in.

The young captain presented himself and Galtieri passed across the report from Garcia in Paris. "This one is highly sensitive, Martinez. Get your book and I'll dictate a brief account of the affair so far, my discussion with General Dozo, and the action we have taken."

"Copies for General Dozo and Admiral Anaya, General, as usual?"

Galtieri shook his head. "General Dozo knows already and the Admiral doesn't deserve to know. One copy for my personal file. Mark it for the eyes of the President only."

"Very well, General."

Carmela Balbuena was a formidable lady in her fifties. Her husband, an Army captain, had been killed seven years previously during the so-called dirty war waged between the government and the back-country guerrillas. She had been on the staff at the Presidential Palace ever since and was now senior secretary.

The report on the Exocet affair was handed over to her by Martinez personally. "I think you'd better do this one yourself, then straight into his personal file, no copy," he said.

She took pride in her work, typing it out meticulously on three sheets of paper, making one carbon copy despite what Martinez had said.

She took the report and showed it to him. "Excellent, Señora. You've excelled yourself. You can file it later, when he's out."

"I'll put it into the office safe till morning. May I go now? I don't think there is anything else."

"Of course. See you in the morning."

She went back into the other room, tidied her desk, took the copies of the three sheets she had made, folded them neatly and put them in her handbag. Then she left, closing the door behind her.

* * *

Carmela Balbuena had never been able to have children and had lavished a great deal of affection on her nephew, the son of her only brother. A Socialist in her ideas, but no Communist, she hated Galtieri and the military regime that kept him in power, disliked a government that had caused so much repression, been instrumental in bringing about the disappearance of so many thousands of ordinary people. Like her nephew, for example, who appeared to have been wiped off the face of the earth since his arrest at a student rally three years previously.

She'd gone to a cultural evening at the French Embassy and had met Jack Daley, the fresh-faced young American who reminded her so much of her nephew. And Daley had been more than attentive, taking her to concerts, the theater, gradually drawing her out, encouraging her to talk of her work at the palace.

It was wholly platonic, and by the time she discovered he was a commercial attaché at the American Embassy and probably much more, she didn't really care. Anything he wanted, she gave him, which included any information of value from the office.

She phoned him at the Embassy from the first public phone booth she came to on her way home and met him an hour later in the Plaza de Mayo where Juan Peron had been so fond of making speeches in the old days.

They sat on a bench in one of the gardens and she passed him a newspaper containing the copy of the report.

"I won't hold you," she said. "I've read that thing and it's dynamite. I'll see you again."

Jack Daley, who was in reality an agent of the CIA, hurried back to the Embassy to read the report in peace. Having read it, he didn't waste any time. Twenty minutes later it was being encoded and forwarded to Washington. Within two hours of being received there, it was being passed on to Brigadier Charles Ferguson in London by order of the Director of the CIA himself.

7

Raul Montera moved out onto the terrace of the house at Vincent Lopez Floreda and took in the gardens below with a conscious pleasure. Palm trees waved in the slight breeze, water gurgled in the conduits and fountains, and the scent of mimosa was heavy on the air. Beyond the garden wall the Rio de la Plata sparkled like silver in the evening sun.

His mother and Linda were sitting at a table beside a fountain on the lower terrace, and it was the child who saw him first. She cried out in delight and came running toward him, arms outstretched, dressed for riding in jodhpurs and a yellow sweater, hair tied back in a ponytail.

"Papa, we didn't know. We didn't know!"

She clutched him, and he held her very tightly. She smiled up at him, fierce and proud. "You were on the television at Rio Gallegos with General Dozo. I saw you. So did all the girls at school."

"Is that so?"

"And the Skyhawks at Death Valley, we saw that too, and I knew you must be flying one of them."

"Death Valley?" He stopped short. "How did you know about that?"

"Isn't that what the pilots call it, the place where they make their run on the British fleet? Two girls in my class at school have lost brothers." She hugged him again. "Oh, I'm so pleased you're safe. Will you be going back?"

"No, not to Gallegos, but I'm going to France in the morning."

They reached the table. His mother sat watching him calmly, cool, elegant, perfectly groomed as usual, looking fifteen years younger than her seventy years.

"I'm supposed to be going riding," Linda said. "I'll cancel it."

"Nonsense," Donna Elena told her. "Run along now. Your father will be here when you get back."

Linda turned to him. "Promise?"

"On my honor."

She hurried up the steps. Montera turned and reached for Donna Elena's hands. "Mother," he said formally as he kissed them. "It's good to see you."

Her eyes took in every aspect of the face, so finely drawn, the haunted eyes. "Oh God," she whispered. "My dearest boy, what have they done to you?"

She was, by nature, self-sufficient and controlled. She had learned many years before never to give too much of herself away. The result was that they had always enjoyed a highly formalized relationship.

But now she didn't stand on ceremony. She got up

and embraced him fervently. "It's so good to have you back safe, Raul. So good."

"Mama." He hadn't used that term since he was a little boy and felt emotion cloud his eyes.

"Come, sit down. Talk to me."

He lit a cigarette and sprawled back, letting everything go. "This is wonderful."

"So, you're not going back?"

"No."

"I must thank the Virgin for that in some suitable way. A man of your age flying jet planes. What nonsense, Raul. A miracle you are here."

"Yes, it is, when you come to think of it," Montera said. "I'd better light a few candles to someone myself."

"To the Virgin or to Gabrielle?" He frowned warily, and she said impatiently, "Here, give me a cigarette. I'm not a fool, you know. I've seen you on television three times now in that Skyhawk of yours. One can hardly miss the inscription just below the cockpit. Who is she, Raul?"

"The woman I love," he said simply, repeating the words he had used to Lami Dozo.

"Tell me about her."

So he did, pacing up and down the terrace beside her restlessly. When he was finished, she said, "She sounds a remarkable young woman."

"An understatement," Montera told her. "The most extraordinary human being I have ever met. Extraordinary for me, that is. I plunged headfirst into love with her the very first moment. There was no contest. And it isn't just her quite astonishing beauty. There's a joy to her that goes way beyond physical passion." He suddenly laughed out loud, and the lines seemed to vanish from his face—he no longer looked tired. "She's so bloody marvelous in every way, Mama. I always had faith that there was something special about life and she's it."

Donna Elena Llorca de Montera took a deep breath. "There's no more to be said then, is there? I presume I'll be introduced in your own good time. Now, tell me why you're going to France."

"Sorry," he told her. "Top secret. All I can say is that it's for what our President is pleased to call The Cause. He also believes that if I'm successful, it would win us the war."

"And will it?"

"If he believes that, he'll believe anything. The cause." He walked to the edge of the terrace and looked out across the river. "We've lost half our pilots so far, Mama. Half. That's what the newspapers don't tell you. The crowds cry out, wave flags. Galtieri makes speeches, but the reality is the butchery at San Carlos Water."

She stood up and took his arm. "Come, Raul, let's go inside now," and together they went up the steps.

At Cavendish Square, Ferguson was seated at the desk, working his way through the CIA signal for the umpteenth time, when Harry Fox came in carrying a couple of files.

"All here, sir. Everything on Felix Donner."

"Tell me, is Gabrielle still in town or has she gone back to Paris?"

"Still at Kensington Palace Gardens. I was having dinner at Langans last night, and she was there with some friends. Why?"

"I should have thought it obvious, Harry. She was considerably smitten by Raul Montera's charms and he with her. We can put that to good use." He looked at Fox's face and raised a hand. "Don't start getting moral on me, Harry. This is war we're playing at now, not patty cake."

"Yes, well there are days when I definitely would rather be doing something else."

"Never mind that now. Donner. Tell me about him. Just the salient facts."

"Multimillionaire. The Donner Development Corporation has a vast range of interests. Building industry, shipping, electronics, you name it."

"And Donner himself?"

"Very popular media figure. Does a lot for charity. Plenty of photographs of him shaking hands with Prince Philip. It's his start in life that's so interesting. Born in the Australian outback at a place near Darwin called Rum Jungle. Orphaned at an early age. Worked on sheep farms and that sort of thing. Volunteered for the Australian Army in 1950. Served with an artillery unit in Korea. Taken prisoner early in fifty-one. Released at the end of the war, the only survivor of his particular unit."

"And then came to England?"

"That's right. Started in real estate development in a very small way. Really took off in the boom of the sixties."

"And never looked back?"

"That's it, sir. In the circumstances and considering the size of his bank balance, it seems odd that he would involve himself in an affair like this, even for a couple of million pounds."

"Exactly." Ferguson sat looking at the file for a while, frowning. "I really do smell stinking fish here in a big way. First of all there's the Russian connection. How was Nikolai Belov so certain after being approached by Garcia that Donner was the man who could help?"

"True. So what are you saying, sir?"

"That Felix Donner was an orphan, which is very convenient. That every other man who served with him and was taken prisoner in Korea died in captivity. Also very convenient."

There was a long silence. Fox said, "Are you saying what I think you are, sir?"

Ferguson got up and walked to the fire and stood there, looking down into the flames.

Fox said, "He's a highly respected businessman, sir. It doesn't make sense."

"Neither did the Gordon Lonsdale affair, remember? Also a highly respected businessman. A Canadian, to all intents and purposes. Even now, after all these years, there's some doubt as to his real identity."

"Excepting that he was a Russian. A professional agent."

"Exactly."

"Are you suggesting that Felix Donner could be another Lonsdale?"

"It's a possibility, that's all we can say for the moment. All right, so he could just be a thoroughly unscrupulous businessman, out, as our American friends would say, to make a buck. We'll have to see."

"So what do we do, sir, pull him in?"

Ferguson went back to his desk. "Difficult while he's in France. Oh, I could pull strings at high levels, but if we went public it would create one hell of a stink, and we might lose considerable long-term advantage. If we could catch him properly, Harry, we might be able to bring down one hell of a house of cards. All his KGB connections in this country, but only if he is what I think he might be."

"That's right."

"And we don't even know what he's up to. Even Garcia has obviously been kept in the dark there. All he can say is that Donner has guaranteed him Exocets by next week. No, what we need now is someone right on his tail who can keep us informed day by day."

Fox said, "And how on earth can we do that?"

"I should have thought it obvious. The key to this affair is Colonel Raul Montera and our link with Montera is Gabrielle Legrand."

There was silence between them and then Fox said, "On the other hand, Gabrielle doesn't like us very much, sir."

"We'll have to see, won't we? You'd better pull her in."

At that moment, the red phone buzzed. He picked it up quickly. "Ferguson here." He listened, face grave, then said, "Of course, sir," and replaced the receiver.

Fox said, "Trouble?"

"That was the Director-General. It seems the Prime Minister wants to see me."

Donner did not, as a rule, enjoy flying in small aircraft. They were noisy, uncomfortable, and lacking in the more obvious amenities, but he could find no fault with the plane Stavrou had arranged. It was a Navajo Chieftain with an excellent cabin and tables that one could sit at in a civilized way.

They took off from a small, private airfield outside Paris at Brie Comte Robert. The pilot was a man called Rabier, a dark, thin-faced man in his early thirties who, according to Stavrou's information, had left the French Air Force under a cloud. He now ran a small air transport firm and didn't ask questions when the money was right. Exactly what they were looking for.

They came in toward the coast over the Vendée, well south of St. Nazaire. Donner had moved up next to the pilot and Rabier said, "Here's where we land. Place called Lancy. It was a Luftwaffe fighter base during the Second World War. Someone tried to run a flying school from there, which failed. Since then, it's been totally deserted."

Donner pointed to a notation on the map. "What's that mean?"

"Restricted air space. There's an island out there off the coast, Île de Roc. Some sort of military testing range. All it means is keep away. Don't worry, navigation is my strong point."

They landed at Lancy twenty minutes later. There were four hangars and the watchtower was still intact, but the grass between the runways was waist-high and there was an air of desolation to everything.

A black Citroën was parked in front of the old operations building, and Wanda Jones got out as the Navajo taxied toward her. She wore jeans and a leather hunting jacket, her dark hair tied back in place with a silk scarf.

Donner descended the air-stair ladder, slipped an arm about her shoulders, and kissed her. "Where did you get the car?"

"Hired it from a garage in St. Martin. And I think I've found just the place you're looking for. Five miles from here and about as far from the coast." She took some keys from her pocket. "The local estate agent entrusted them to me. I explained that my boss didn't like to be bothered with such matters. I'm certain he thinks I'm setting up a love nest for weekends."

"Looking at you, what else would he think?" Donner told her. "Anyway, let's get moving. You drive, Yanni."

Stavrou got behind the wheel, and Wanda got into

the rear. Donner turned to Rabier who was peering out from the Navajo.

"A couple of hours at the most, I think, then back to Paris."

"Fine by me, Monsieur."

Donner got into the car beside the girl and they drove away.

The house was called Maison Blanc and nestled among beech trees in a hollow. It was quite large and had obviously been imposing once, but now there was a general air of decay about it.

Donner got out of the Citroën and stood at the bottom of the steps, looking up at the front door under the portico with the green paint peeling rather noticeably.

"Fourteen bedrooms and a stable at the rear," Wanda said. "There's reasonably modern central heating and the oil tanks are full. You could manage here for a few days, I think."

"What's the story?"

"The owner is in the colonial service in the Pacific. His mother died two years ago, and as he wants to retire here eventually, he won't sell. It's fully furnished. The agent lets it off for holidays occasionally in the summer, otherwise it stands empty."

She unlocked the door and led the way in. There was a slight musty smell, typical of a house not lived in for a long time, but there was a kind of faded magnificence to everything. Lots of mahogany paneling and furniture and good Persian carpets on the floor.

They moved into an enormous sitting room with a huge fireplace and a chandelier. Wanda opened the French windows and then the outside shutters, allowing light to flood in.

"All the comforts of home. Imagine it with the central heating going and a log fire. Haven't I done well?"

"Excellent," Donner said. "Take it."

"I already have."

He pulled her into his arms. "You're a clever little bitch, aren't you?"

"Some of the time. I aim to please."

As always, she stirred him physically, which wouldn't do at all, for this was neither the time nor place. He kissed her once and turned away.

"Right, show me St. Martin. Is it possible to see Île de Roc?"

"On the horizon and only if the weather's good."

"Let's get going then."

He went out. As she turned to follow, she was aware of Stavrou, watching her as he always seemed to, that enigmatic face, and yet the eyes so cruel and with something in them especially for her. She hurried past him quickly, and he followed her out.

St. Martin was a simple enough place. No more than five or six hundred inhabitants, narrow cobbled streets, cottages roofed with red pantiles, a small harbor enclosed by a single breakwater in which thirty or forty fishing boats of the smaller variety were moored.

There was also an army landing craft painted olive green and moored to the jetty—little more than a steel shell with great steel bow doors as a beaching exit. An army truck stood inside, and as they watched, the craft moved away from the jetty and out to sea.

"So that's their main means of transportation to the island," Donner said.

Wanda nodded. "Apparently."

"According to Paul Bernard, the commanding officer out there also has a rather fine motor launch, which is his personal pride and joy."

"That's right. It was moored down there for a while yesterday."

"Good. That's really excellent."

They drove on, up out of the town, following a narrow coast road until finally Stavrou, under Wanda's direction, turned in through two stone pillars and bumped across a field track.

Donner and Wanda got out and she handed him a pair of Zeiss field glasses as they went forward to the edge of the cliffs. There was a bay far below, and the path down was no place for the faint-hearted, zigzagging across the face of granite cliffs, splashed with lime, seabirds crying, wheeling in great clouds, razorbills, shags, gulls, shearwaters, and gannets—gannets everywhere.

Île de Roc was a smudge on the horizon that came to life only when he focused the glasses. It was well named, massive cliffs rising steeply from the sea, only a hint of green on top. There were no installations to be seen, but he already knew they were on the western side of the island.

He lowered the glasses. "Good, let's go."

They returned to the Citroën, got in, and Stavrou reversed and drove away.

On the way back, they passed Maison Blanc again. A few hundred yards on, as they turned into the road leading to Lancy, Donner leaned forward and touched Stavrou on the shoulder.

"Stop a minute. What have we got here?"

In the meadow beside the trees, three wagons were parked around a fire. They were old and battered, with patched canvas awnings. A depressing air of poverty hung over everything from the ragged clothes worn by the four women who squatted by the fire drinking coffee from old cans, to the ragged clothing of the children, who played by the stream where three bony horses grazed.

"Gypsies?" Donner asked.

"Yes, the agent said there were some in the neighborhood. Said they were no trouble."

"He would, wouldn't he?" Donner nodded to Stavrou. "Come on, Yanni, this may work out quite well."

As they walked down into the hollow, the women looked up curiously, saying nothing. Donner stood there, hands in pockets, then said in French, "Where's the head man?"

"Here he is, Monsieur."

The man who had appeared from the trees was old, at least seventy. He had a shotgun crooked in his right arm. He wore an old tweed suit patched many times and white hair showed beneath the blue beret. His face was the color of oak, wrinkled and covered with white stubble.

"And who might you be?" Donner inquired.

"I am Paul Gaubert, Monsieur. Is it permitted to ask you the same question?"

"My name is Donner. I'm the new tenant of Maison Blanc. I think I'm probably right in saying you're camped on my land."

"But Monsieur, we stay here every year at this time. Never before have we had a problem."

The young man with him was of medium height with a weak, sullen face that badly needed a shave. His clothes were as shabby as Gaubert's. Black hair poked from beneath a tweed cap. He not only carried a shotgun in his right hand, but a brace of hares in his left.

Donner looked him over and Gaubert said hastily, "My son, Paul."

"With my hares, I think? What would the local gendarmes in St. Martin have to say about your lot, I wonder?"

Old Gaubert flung his arms wide. "Please, Monsieur, everywhere we go it is the same. Filthy gypsies, they say. They spit on us while our children go hungry."

"All right." Donner took out his wallet. "I don't need the sob story. You can stay." He took out a couple of thousand-franc notes and stuffed them into Gaubert's breast pocket. "That's to be going on with. I don't like strangers, understand?"

The old man took out the notes, examined them, and smiled broadly. "I think so, Monsieur."

"Just keep an eye on things till I'm back down again, or Monsieur Stavrou here."

"You can rely on me, Monsieur," old Gaubert said and kicked his son on the leg for gawping at Wanda, who stood further up the slope watching.

They went back to the Citroën and as they drove away she said, "Now what?"

"Paris. I've got to make arrangements about this Argentine pilot. Montera. Garcia tells me he's flown twelve missions to the Falklands and survived."

"An authentic hero," she said. "I thought they'd gone out of style."

"So did I, but this guy is for real and he's going to suit my purpose admirably. By the time I'm finished with him, he'll be world famous."

He slipped an arm about her shoulders and leaned back in the seat.

8

At that time, because of the Falklands situation, unusually large crowds had started to congregate in Downing Street and the police had been compelled to cordon off most of the street.

When Ferguson showed his special pass, his car was allowed to go through and drop him outside Number 10, five minutes early for his appointment with the Prime Minister. The policeman on duty saluted, the door was opened even before Ferguson reached it, and he passed inside.

The young aide who greeted him said, "This way, Brigadier, the Prime Minister is expecting you."

Ferguson followed him up the main staircase, not for the first time in his career, past the portraits of previous Prime Ministers—Peel, Wellington, Disraeli, Gladstone. It always filled him with an acute sense of history, and he wondered whether the woman who held the most august office in the land was similarly affected. Probably so. If anyone had a sense of history and destiny, she did. He doubted whether the entire Falklands venture could have gone forward without her strength of purpose and courage behind it.

In the top corridor, the young man knocked on a door, opened it and ushered Ferguson inside. "Brigadier Ferguson, Prime Minister," he said and left, closing the door.

The study was just as elegant as when Ferguson had last seen it, with pale green walls and gold curtains and comfortable furniture in excellent taste. But as always, nothing could have been more elegant than the woman behind the desk in the neat blue suit and white blouse, the blonde hair perfectly groomed.

She looked at him calmly. "The last time we had dealings, Brigadier, was in connection with a possible attempt on my life."

"Yes, ma'am."

"Your efforts on that occasion were not conspicuously successful. If the would-be assassin had not thought better of the matter here in this very room . . ."

She let her words hang for a while and then carried on. "I see that the Director-General of Intelligence has seen fit, in his wisdom, to place you in charge of all matters relating to the Exocet question."

"Yes, ma'am."

"I understand that the Libyans had intended to provide the Argentinians with additional supplies, but thanks to pressure from our friends in the Arab world, this is no longer likely?"

'That is correct, Prime Minister."

"Is there any possibility that the Peruvians might try to help?"

'That contingency has already been taken care of ma'am. We . . ."

"Please, Brigadier, spare me the details. Which only leaves the French, and I have Monsieur Mitterand's personal assurance that the arms embargo will stay in force."

"I'm pleased to hear it, ma'am."

She stood up, walked to the window, and looked out. "Brigadier, if one Exocet hits either *Hermes* or *Invincible,* the entire course of this conflict is changed. We would almost certainly have to withdraw." She turned. "Can you assure me that there is no possibility of further Exocets reaching Argentina from any source whatever?"

"No, ma'am, I'm afraid I can't."

"Then I suggest you do something about that, Brigadier," she said calmly. "Group Four has full power— total authority from this office. Use it, Brigadier, use it any way you can, for the sake of our men in the South Atlantic, for all our sakes."

"Thank you, Prime Minister. I'll do my best, I can assure you of that."

Ferguson got the door open and went out. The eyes of those previous Prime Ministers seemed to follow him as he went down the stairs. He wondered if he'd just secured himself a small niche in history, but decided probably not. Even if it all worked perfectly, it was exactly the kind of thing they'd all deny had happened afterward. He chuckled to himself as the aide bowed him to the front door and showed him out.

As Harry Fox and Ferguson went up in the elevator at Kensington Palace Gardens, Fox said, "We're wasting our time, sir. When I tried to speak to her on the phone, she just told me to get lost."

"We'll see," Ferguson said.

He pushed open the elevator door, went around the corner to Gabrielle's flat, and knocked. After a while, the door opened on the chain and she peered out.

"What do you want?"

"To talk to you."

"Well I don't want to talk to you. Clear off!"

She started to close the door and he pushed his foot in. "Not even about Raul Montera?"

She stared blankly at him, then took off the chain and turned away. Ferguson followed her in, and Fox closed the door behind them.

She went and stood by the fire and lit one of her rare cigarettes. "Well, get on with it."

She looked magnificent in her anger, eyes full of hate, and Ferguson decided to go in with both feet.

"Raul Montera arrives in Paris tomorrow to liaise with a man called Felix Donner who the Argentine government believes can procure them an additional supply of Exocet missiles. I need to find out what they're up to and stop them. I want you to go to Paris,

110

make contact with Montera again, and do whatever is necessary to help us stop them cold."

"You must be crazy. I'll never work for you again. Never."

"It's your duty. You're still a British citizen."

"I am also a citizen of France. That makes me neutral."

"Impossible," he said calmly. "Your half brother, Sublieutenant Richard Brindsley, is serving as helicopter pilot on board HMS *Invincible,* as you very well know."

"Stop it!" she said desperately. "I won't listen."

"He is serving with 820 Squadron," Ferguson carried on relentlessly. "The same squadron as His Royal Highness, Prince Andrew. Let me tell you what one of his more unpleasant duties is. The Sea Kings are frequently used to act as decoys for Exocet missiles. Prince Andrew and your brother and their comrades act in the belief that an Exocet cannot fly above twenty-seven feet. They hover, presenting an attractive radar target, protecting the ships of the fleet. At the last moment possible, the idea is to gain height quickly so that the missile passes beneath them. Unfortunately, rogue Exocets have been known to exceed that height. I'll spare you a description of the possibilities."

She was almost beside herself with rage and fear. "I won't listen. Leave me alone."

"And then there's your friend, Montera. A gallant fool if ever I saw one, but the enemy in this war,

Gabrielle, make no mistake about that. A man who has flown a Skyhawk with a five-thousand-pound bomb load to attack the British fleet in San Carlos Water on no fewer than twelve occasions. I wonder which frigate he helped sink?"

She turned away. Ferguson nodded to Fox and went out. Fox followed, closed the door, and found him in the elevator, his face strained.

"I told you it was a waste of time."

"Nonsense," Ferguson said. "She'll go." As the elevator descended he said, "She'll need a man, Harry, to back her up. Someone totally dependable and quite ruthless. You do know where Tony is at this precise moment of time?"

"Operating behind the Argentinian lines somewhere in the Falklands with the SAS."

"Right. I thought I might need him so I sent a signal last night, utmost priority. I want him pulled out. Picked up by submarine and offloaded into Uruguay. It's only fourteen hours by plane from Montevideo to Paris. Our people at the Embassy in Montevideo can have the necessary papers waiting for him."

"All right, sir, but what will Gabrielle say?"

"Gabrielle?"

"It won't make her feel any better to have her ex-husband peering over her shoulder while she's spying on her lover."

"It can't be helped. Villiers not only knows Gabrielle, he knows how she thinks. It's too late, Harry, to put a new man on this thing. If you think I'm going to send in someone to run the show who knows neither Gabrielle nor Montera, you're mistaken."

They went out and down the steps toward the car. He said, "I know, Harry, don't bother to say it. I'm the great original bastard of all time."

Belov and Garcia sat with Donner in the study of his apartment and waited while Wanda poured coffee.

"That's fine," Donner said to her. "Any business calls from the corporation in London, you handle and tell Yanni to stand by. I may need him."

She went out and he said to Garcia, "So, Colonel Montera arrives tomorrow? You've brought me that file on him I asked for, I trust? I like to know who I'm dealing with."

"Of course." Garcia opened his briefcase and produced a small folder, which he pushed across.

Donner opened it, studied the photo it contained of Montera, and quickly scanned the details on the sheets.

"Excellent," he said at last. "What arrangements have you made as regards accommodation?"

"A hotel didn't seem like a good idea," Garcia said. "And certainly not the Embassy. I've leased a small service flat for him in an apartment block on the avenue de Neuilly by the Bois de Boulogne." He passed a card across. "There's the address and telephone number."

"Good." Donner nodded. "I'll make the necessary contact with him once he arrives."

Garcia said, "I was wondering when we might have

some further details as to exactly what you intend." There was a kind of exasperation in his voice. "I mean, you've still given us not the slightest hint where you expect to get the Exocets from."

"And I don't intend to," Donner said. "Not until the very last moment. This is a matter of the utmost delicacy. The fewer people who know my source, the better. I'm sorry but that's the way I work." He shrugged. "Of course if you're not satisfied, it would still be possible to pull out."

"Good God, no," Garcia said hastily. "I didn't mean that, not for a moment."

"I'm glad to hear it. Now, if you wouldn't mind leaving us alone for a moment. You can wait in the next room. I'm sure Wanda can find you some more coffee."

Garcia went out. Belov said, "Amateurs. What on earth is one supposed to do with them?"

"Keep them out of harm's way, that's what," Donner said. "I've already made it plain to Paul Bernard that under no circumstances does he discuss with Garcia his dealings with me."

"Who therefore knows nothing about your interest in Île de Roc?"

"Exactly."

"And can you trust Bernard?"

"Oh, yes, the good professor has really got the bit between his teeth now. Looks upon the whole thing as a kind of holy crusade. I haven't been explicit, but he obviously thinks I intend to hijack one of the Aérospatiale trucks that transport Exocets by road to the island every so often. Mind you, if he knew my exact intentions, he might not be so pleased. But he has served my purpose very well."

"And what happens to him afterward?"

"Something suitably dramatic, I think, like being found dead with a gun in one hand and a suicide note, regretting his involvement in a conspiracy against his own country to obtain Exocets for the Argentine government. French Intelligence will have little difficulty in establishing that he gave all that technical assistance early in the campaign. According to Garcia, he was on the telephone to Buenos Aires answering queries for lengthy periods on a number of occasions. It should all come out very satisfactorily. France is, after all, a democracy. Three cheers for a free press."

"You really do think of everything, don't you?"

"I try. Now to something you can help me with. I need an address where I can pick up some muscle."

"How many men?"

"I'd say about eight, which makes ten with me and Stavrou. Ample for my purposes if they are the right breed. Thoroughgoing hoods. Nothing fancy about using their brains. The kind of men who will kill if the price is right."

"There's always the Union Corse," Belov said.

The Union Corse was, of course, the largest crime syndicate in France, a truly formidable organization whose tentacles reached out everywhere from the judiciary to the government itself.

Donner shook his head. "I don't think so. They

may be gangsters, those boys, but they're inclined to be patriotic. The curse of the French, Nikolai, or hadn't you noticed? Even the Communist variety look upon themselves as Frenchmen first."

"Point taken," Belov said. "But we do have other contacts. You could really do with mercenaries rather than ordinary gangsters."

"Or gangsters who've seen service in the army. God knows, there must still be plenty of those around in France after all those years in Algiers."

"Leave it to me."

Donner opened a drawer, took out a sheet of paper, and passed it across. "I'll also need the items on there."

Belov examined the list and raised his eyebrows. "You intend to go to war, to judge from this little lot?"

"You could put it that way."

At that moment, the door opened and Juan Garcia entered. He was trembling with excitement, eyes shining. "What is it, for God's sake?" Belov demanded.

"Today, gentlemen, is the twenty-fifth of May. You know what that means in Argentina?"

"I can't say I do."

"It is our national day, a day that will go down in our history as one on which we dealt the British Navy the most crushing blow of the war. It's on now, a news flash on television. Come and see," and he turned and hurried out.

* * *

In the office at Cavendish Square, Ferguson put down the red phone, his face grave.

Harry Fox said, "Is it bad, sir?"

"You could say that. The destroyer HMS *Coventry,* while protecting vessels landing supplies at San Carlos, was attacked by Skyhawks. She may also have been hit by an Exocet, we aren't sure yet. At least twenty dead and many wounded. She capsized."

"My God," Fox said.

"There's worse, Harry. The fifteen-thousand-ton container ship, *Atlantic Conveyor,* has also been taken out. Two Exocet hits definitely confirmed." He shook his head. "Because of her size on the radar screen, they probably thought she was one of the aircraft carriers."

There was silence for a while, only the muted sounds of traffic from outside in the square. Fox said, "What do we do now, sir?"

"I think that's obvious," Ferguson told him. "Don't you?"

When he knocked at the door of the flat in Kensington Palace Gardens for the second time that day, there was a delay before slow steps approached and the door opened on the chain.

Gabrielle looked out. She stared at them for a long moment, then opened the door and led the way into the sitting room. She was wearing the old bathrobe and looked dreadful, her hair tousled, eyes swollen.

"You've heard the news?" Ferguson asked gently.

She nodded. "Yes."

"And?"

She took a deep breath and folded her arms as if holding herself together. "When do you want me to go?"

"Tomorrow, I think. You still have the apartment on the avenue Victor Hugo?"

"Yes."

"Good. Get yourself settled in. You'll be informed what to do by our man in Paris, or if necessary Harry can go over on the shuttle to see you. And there is one more thing."

She looked incredibly weary now. "And what would that be?"

"You'll need a backup man. Someone totally reliable, to be on hand in case you get into trouble."

Her eyes widened in a kind of horror. "You've sent for Tony?"

"That's right. He should be here in thirty-six hours at the outside."

She shook her head helplessly. "I'd like to kill you, Ferguson. I've never wished death on any human being in my life, but I'd really relish seeing you dead. You corrupt everything you touch."

"Harry will make your travel arrangements," he said. "He'll be in touch. Take a couple of pills, get some sleep. You'll feel better for it."

When they went outside, it had started to rain. Ferguson paused to button up his coat and Fox said, "Can she handle it, sir? It's expecting a hell of a lot. I mean, the impression I get is that she's head over heels in love with Raul Montera."

118

"Yes, an interesting situation," Ferguson said. "But we don't really have any choice, do we?" He glanced up at the rain and raised his collar as he went down the steps. "All of a sudden I feel old, Harry. What do you think about that? Very, very old."

In Buenos Aires, the plaza in front of the National Congress Building was crammed with thousands of excited people, hundreds of blue and white Argentinian flags waving everywhere.

Above the hooting of car horns, the crowd roared: *Argentina! Argentina!* On a balcony in full uniform, silver hair swept back, arm raised in salute like a Roman emperor, Galtieri took the plaudits of the crowd.

And then the voices changed, became a chorus like the sea rushing in, carrying everything before it, and the word that they repeated over and over again, like a litany, was Exocet.

Ferguson was sitting by the fire in the flat toasting crumpets when Fox came in with a cable in his hand.

"Oh, I wanted to see you, Harry. Who have we got at the Paris Embassy who isn't a complete idiot?"

Fox thought about it. "George Corwin is a possibility, sir. Was a captain in the Green Howards when we recruited him. Did quite well in Ireland. His mother is French, that's why we posted him to Paris."

"Excellent. He can pick Montera up when he arrives from Buenos Aires. Find out where he's staying and liaise with Gabrielle till Tony gets in. Talking about Tony, what's happening there?"

"I was just bringing this cable to you, sir. Text of a message from H.Q. at San Carlos via SAS headquarters at Hereford."

"What's it say?"

"Confirm Major Villiers and Sergeant Major Jackson en route as ordered."

"I wonder how Tony took it, being hauled out of the action like that."

"I shouldn't imagine he'd be too pleased," Fox said.

"Well that would make sense, knowing our Tony," Ferguson said. "After all, it's the only war he's got."

9

And on the day previously it had been a quiet morning at first light in the mountains of East Falkland, the only sound a dog barking from one of the farms far, far below in a valley.

The four-man SAS reconnaissance team, put ashore by submarine, had been operating behind the Argentine lines for ten days now, since before the British landings at San Carlos on the twenty-first.

The team consisted of Villiers, Harvey Jackson, the radio operator, a Corporal Elliot of the Royal Corps of Signals, and the fourth member of the group, a trooper named Jack Korda, a volunteer to the SAS from the Grenadier Guards, like Villiers and Jackson.

It was bitterly cold. When Villiers had first awakened he had found his sleeping poncho covered with hoarfrost. He stood now in the hollow beside a small cave, not much more than a fissure in the rocks, inside which Korda was heating tea on a small chemical stove.

Villiers, like the others, wore a black woolen balaclava, more against the cold than anything else. His camouflage uniform was soaking wet, his fingers numb with cold as he ate from a mess can with a spoon. Jackson sat cross-legged on the ground, a guardsman to the end, and scraped shaving foam from his chin with a plastic razor.

Villiers's spoon rattled against the bottom of the mess can. He stowed it away in his pack and accepted the mug of tea Korda passed out to him.

"I've had enough chicken supreme to last me a lifetime. How about you, Harvey?"

"Oh, it keeps me going as well as anything else," Jackson said. "Food's not all that important. When I was seventeen the food in the guardsmen's mess at the depot was so awful, I've never been able to take it seriously since."

Elliot was crouched by the radio, and Villiers moved across. "Everything okay?"

Elliot glanced up and nodded. "Through in a minute."

The patrol's task was simple enough. To pick up as much information as possible about Argentinian troop movements in the area. Information that would be of the utmost importance when British forces broke out from the San Carlos beachhead.

The equipment Elliot carried was of the very latest kind. There was a small typewriter-style keyboard, and through this system messages could be entered and stored in code. When Elliot was ready, the touch of a button was sufficient to send a message of a few hundred words in a matter of seconds. They were on the air so briefly that it was impossible for the enemy to have any hope of tracing them.

Elliot looked up and grinned. "That's it." He started to pack his equipment.

Korda crawled out of the fissure with more tea. "When do we go in, sir? How much longer?"

"Rations for four more days," Villiers reminded him.

"Which means we can last a week," Harvey Jackson said. "Longer, if you don't mind raw mutton. Sheep all over the place. The Argies have been doing very nicely on that diet."

Before Korda could reply, Villiers said, "Just a minute. Something coming."

There was a murmur in the distance that grew louder, and Villiers and the others crawled forward cautiously to the edge of the hollow and peered over. They each carried the same weapon, the silenced version of the Sterling submachine gun.

An Argentinian truck was approaching along the rough track about a hundred yards away, its front wheels spinning on the frozen ground, only the half-tracks at the rear keeping it going.

The driver and the man who sat beside him in the front seat, with a rifle across his knees, were muffled up to their ears against the intense cold, scarves bound around their faces.

"Sitting ducks," Elliot said. "Even if there's somebody in the rear."

But the patrol's task was to seek information, not confrontation. Villiers said, "No, let them go."

And then the truck slithered to a halt, half slewed across the track directly below them.

"Watch it!" Villiers said.

As they all crouched low the driver jumped down from behind the wheel and Villiers heard him say in Spanish, "This stinking engine again with the stinking oil that isn't supposed to freeze and turns into lumps instead. What are we doing in this place?"

He raised the hood to examine the engine, and his friend got out, still holding his rifle, and lit a cigarette.

"Okay, ease off," Villiers whispered.

They started to slide back from the rim. Korda put out a hand to steady himself, but rock and soil broke away suddenly and slid down the slope to the track below, gathering momentum.

The two Argentine soldiers cried out in alarm. The one with the rifle swung around, raising it instinctively, and Harvey Jackson, having no choice, jumped up and cut him down with the silenced Sterling. The only sound was the bolt reciprocating. The Argentinian's rifle flew into the air, and he fell back against the truck.

The driver got his hands in the air fast and stood waiting as the four men went down the slope. Korda banged him against the truck, legs spread, and Jackson searched him with ruthless efficiency.

"Nothing," he said to Villiers and turned the soldier around.

He was only a boy, no more than seventeen or eighteen, and frightened to death.

"What's in the back?" Villiers demanded in Spanish.

"Supplies, equipment," the boy said, eager to please. "Nothing more, Señor, I swear it. Please don't kill me."

"All right," Villiers nodded to Jackson. "Take a look."

He lit a cigarette and gave one to the boy, whose hand shook as he accepted a light. The fear in him was so strong you could almost smell it.

Jackson came back. "Must be sappers. Lots of land mines in there, explosives, and so on."

Villiers said to the Argentinian, "You're with an engineering unit?"

"No," the boy said. "Transport. The men I took to Bull Cove last night, I think they were engineers."

Bull Cove was a place Villiers and the patrol knew well. One of their first tasks on arrival had been to survey the area as a possible site to put more troops ashore behind the Agentinian lines when the push started from San Carlos. The cove had proved an admirable choice — well protected from the sea with a deepwater channel through a narrow entrance, above which stood a disused lighthouse. Villiers had sent in a favorable report.

"How many of them were there?"

"An officer and two men, Señor. A Captain Lopez. They unloaded a lot of equipment and then the captain decided he needed some special fuses." He took a crumpled list from his pocket. "See, here it is, Señor. He was sending me back to base for these things."

Jackson looked over Villiers's shoulders. "Kaden pencils. That's pretty heavy stuff. What in the hell does he want that for?"

"To blow up the lighthouse, Senor," the boy said patiently. "And rocks, also, I think."

"To blow up the lighthouse?" Jackson said.

The boy nodded. "Oh yes, Señor, I heard them discussing it."

"Rubbish," Jackson said. "Why go to the trouble? It hasn't been used for thirty years. Doesn't make sense."

"Oh yes it does, Harvey," Villiers said. "Especially if you consider its position on the rocks above the entrance. Bring it down there and you'll efficiently block the only deepwater channel into the cove."

"Christ," Jackson said. "Then we'd better do something about it and fast." He said to the boy in bad Spanish, "How far is it from here on this road?"

"Fifteen or sixteen kilometers around the mountain."

"Only not in this, not any more." Villiers kicked the halftrack. There was a strong smell of gasoline, which dripped from the tank in a steady flow, melting the frozen ground. "You did a pretty thorough job, Harvey."

Jackson swore savagely. "So what in the hell do we do?"

Villiers turned and looked up at the mountain towering into the mist. "Bull Cove's directly on the other side. Say six miles. We'll do it the hard way. You, me, Korda. Leave all equipment behind. Sterlings only. Now you'll find out what all that endurance testing on the Brecons was all about."

They went back to the hidden encampment, Jackson pushing the boy along in front of him. As Villiers stripped his excess gear, he said to Elliot, "You follow with the boy. Don't bother about this stuff. Just bring the radio and your own gear."

"Very well, sir."

"And the kid," Villiers said. "I want him to arrive with you. No stories about how he made a run for it and you had to cut him down, understand?"

"Do I look as if I'd do a thing like that, sir?" Elliot demanded.

"Yes," Jackson said sourly, "so don't. I'll give you two-and-a-half hours to join us and let you choose an easy route out of consideration to the kid. Five minutes over and I'll have your guts for garters."

"All right," Villiers said. "Let's go, you two," and he turned, moved out of the hollow, and started to run across the hillside.

It has been said that out of every fifty soldiers who volunteer for transfer to the Special Air Service Regiment, only one makes the grade, and the culmination of a savage and punishing selection procedure is the endurance march across the wilderness that is the Brecon Beacons.

The would-be recruit for Britain's most elite corps

is required to march forty-five miles across some of the worst country, loaded down with a belt kit weighing probably fifteen pounds. And his eighteen-pound rifle has to be carried because SAS weapons are not allowed slings so that they are always available for instant use.

Scrambling up through the mist now, Villiers was reminded of his own selection purgatory when he'd first volunteered. Jackson came up beside him, panting.

"Just like sodding Brecon. All it has to do is rain and we'll be right at home. Why all the rush? I mean if the kid was sent for more stuff, they must be taking their time."

"Bad feeling," Villiers said. "Right down in the gut. You know me. Always right when I get that."

"Enough said," Jackson replied and turned and called to Korda, who was twenty yards behind. "Come on, you lazy bastard, move it!"

Instead of working his way diagonally up the steep hillside, Villiers went straight up, and the others followed him. The slope lifted until it was almost perpendicular, with rough frozen tussocks of grass sticking out of bare rock.

As they came to the foot of an apron of loose stone and shale, he paused and glanced back at his companions.

"Okay?"

"No, bloody awful, actually," Jackson said.

Korda said, "The things I do for England. My old mum will be so proud."

"You never had one, son," Jackson said.

As they started forward, it began to rain a little. "Watch it," Villiers said. "A bit treacherous from here on in."

He stuffed the Sterling inside the tunic of his camouflage uniform and zipped it up. Awkward, but it left his hands free. Once, he heaved strongly on a boulder, and it tore free, and he swung quickly to one side, crying a warning. It bounced and crashed its way down the mountainside, disappearing into the mist.

"You two all right?"

"Only just," Jackson called.

Villiers started to climb again, and a moment later he found himself standing on the edge of a broad plateau. Jackson and Korda joined him.

"Now what?" Jackson demanded.

Villiers pointed across the plateau to the great rock wall that faced them, draped in mist. Fissures and cracks branched across it in dark fingers. He led the way across the plateau at a jog trot, picking his way between boulders. When they reached the base of the rock, it became apparent that it wasn't actually perpendicular, but tilted back slightly in great slabs.

"Dear God," Korda said, looking up.

"He helps those who help themselves," Jackson said. "So let's get moving."

Villiers led the way, climbing strongly, concentrating on the rock in front of him, not looking down, for a secret he had nursed to himself for years was his fear of heights. If the selection board had known that, he would never have served in the 22 SAS, that was for certain.

He paused at one point, braced against the rock, and for a moment seemed to float in space. It was as if a giant hand were trying to pull him away.

"You okay, sir?" Jackson called.

It broke the spell. Villiers nodded and started to climb again, forgetting his aching limbs, the icy wind, his numbed hands. He moved at last over a tilted slab and found himself on a broad ledge. Above him, a wall of rock lifted a hundred feet, no more, and beyond it was only gray sky.

He waited for the others to join him, which they did a couple of minutes later.

"Jesus, not some more," Jackson said.

Villiers indicated a dark chimney that cut its way straight up through the solid rock. "Looks bad, but it's the easiest part of the climb."

"I'll take your word for it," Jackson said.

Villiers pulled himself up into the gloom then turned and, using the common mountaineering technique, braced his back against one wall and feet against the other, resting every fifteen or twenty feet, his body firmly wedged.

After a while he found it was possible to climb properly and the handholds were good and plentiful. Ten minutes later, he scrambled over the edge.

The wind cut like a knife and the rain, at that

level, had turned to sleet. He pulled on his gloves again, stamping his feet against the bitter cold, and eventually Jackson joined him and then Korda. They looked tired and drawn and the balaclava helmets were covered with frost.

The mountains sloped down toward the sea, wrapped in gray mist and low cloud. Suddenly, the wind tore a hole in the curtain, and for a moment only they had a glimpse of the Atlantic and far, far below, the tiny bay and the white finger of the old lighthouse standing at the entrance.

"There she is. Bull Cove," Villiers said as the curtain dropped back into place. "Let's get moving."

He pulled the Sterling out of his tunic, held it across his chest with both hands, and started to run down the mountainside.

Captain Carlos Lopez carefully uncoiled the wire he had just taped to the charge he had positioned on the second floor and paused to light a cigarette. All five floors linked now, which left only the ground. It had progressed faster than he had anticipated, and he was whistling cheerfully as he started down the stairs, uncoiling the wire behind him.

Once at ground level, he ran the wire across to the center of the floor, where a large, blue cylinder stood ready. He removed the lid very carefully. Inside there were various terminals and two buttons, one yellow, the other red. Very carefully, he clipped the wires into position, sat back satisfied, then gently depressed the yellow button.

He glanced up and smiled. "One hour, baby, then the big bang."

There was a rattle of small-arms fire close at hand, and, as Lopez turned, Private Olivera appeared in the doorway.

"British troops coming down the hill."

"How many?"

"I counted three."

There was no sound and yet suddenly blood spurted as Olivera was driven forward through the doorway in a mad dance to fall face down, his quilted parka starting to smolder.

Lopez snatched up an Uzi submachine gun and ran to the door, crouching, and waited.

It had been sheer bad luck that Carvallo, the third Argentinian, had been sitting in the shelter of an old sheep pen some little way up the hillside. Its rusting corrugated iron roof had afforded shelter from the rain while he smoked a cigarette and wrote a letter home to his girl friend in Bahia Blanca.

He stretched, stood up, and walked out of the entrance. To his total astonishment he saw the three SAS men approaching cautiously along the track, keeping to the wall.

They became aware of him in the same instant. He snatched up his machine pistol and loosed off a wild burst that went skyward as Jackson and Korda fired together, driving him back into the sheep pen.

"Now!" Villiers cried. "And fast!"

Korda went straight down the track, Jackson to the left, Villiers to the right. They broke from cover, running headlong, very fast, in time to see Olivera run into the entrance of the lighthouse and stand there for a moment. Villiers and Korda both fired, sending Olivera staggering inside.

Villiers dropped to one knee to reload and Korda kept right on going, straight down the track into the open.

"No!" Villiers shouted, and Lopez fired a long burst around the edge of the door, knocking Korda off his feet.

The boy lay there for a moment, then turned over and tried to crawl. Lopez fired around the door again, the rounds kicking up fountains of dirt close to Korda's head.

Jackson ran to join him, loosing off a long burst that raked the doorway, and then his Sterling jammed, owing to overheating, a tendency of the weapon when used too much with the silencer.

Jackson grabbed the boy by the scruff of the neck and pulled him into the flimsy shelter of an old water trough. In the lighthouse, Lopez shoved another clip into his Uzi and raked the trough with several bursts until water spouted from a dozen holes.

Villiers unscrewed the silencer on his Sterling, rammed home a fresh clip, and went down the hill on the run, running right across the front of the lighthouse, loosing off the entire magazine in one long continuous burst. As the gun emptied, he dived headfirst into sodden bracken and rolled over, reaching for the Smith & Wesson magnum he carried in the pouch on his right leg.

And Lopez, hearing the Sterling empty itself, bought it, jumping out of the entrance, the Uzi raised to fire. Villiers shot him in the left shoulder, spinning him around, the Uzi jumping into the air.

The Argentinian slid down the wall as Villiers approached and kicked the Uzi to one side. "Very good," Lopez said. "I congratulate you."

Villiers opened a pouch on his left leg, took out a field service dressing pack and broke it open. "Here, hold this on it."

He turned and crossed to the water trough. Korda lay sprawled against it, face twisted with pain. Jackson applied a field service dressing to his left thigh.

"He'll live," Jackson said. "Though he doesn't deserve to. Daft bastard," he said as he jabbed a morphine capsule into Korda's arm. "Who did you think you were, Audie Murphy?"

"Who's he?" Korda asked weakly.

"Never mind."

Jackson gave him a cigarette, then followed Villiers back to the lighthouse and Lopez.

"Watch him," Villiers said and slipped into the entrance.

His practiced eye took in the blue cylindrical box, the wires disappearing up the spiral staircase. He turned, "A charge on every floor, all linked?"

"Of course, my friend. If your people hoped to use this harbor they'd better think again. When this baby blows, she drops straight into the entrance. I know my business."

"What did you send the truck back for Kaden pencils for?"

"I was going to bring down some cliff face as well."

"Good job we got here when we did then," Villiers said.

"Touch that box and find out. It's on a timer." Lopez glanced at his watch, face streaked with pain. "Forty-five minutes to go, but there's an anti-handling device that sends the whole thing off instantly if you touch."

"Is that a fact?" Villiers nodded to Jackson. "Bring him in, Harvey."

He went inside and squatted beside the blue box. Jackson helped Lopez in and eased the Argentinian down on the floor. He sat there, pressing the dressing against his wound.

Villiers said, "I've seen one of these things before, but only in a manual. Russian, isn't it?"

"That's right."

"So you depressed the yellow button that controls the timer and, as you say, the damn thing is lethal if I attempt to unplug it." He took a pack of cigarettes from his pocket and stuck one in the corner of his mouth. "And this red button, as I recall, cuts into the circuit."

"You know your stuff."

"Circumventing the timer and giving us three minutes to get out, isn't that so?"

He depressed the red button and Lopez said, "Holy Mother of God."

"It's up to you," Villiers told him. "I presume you know how to stop it?" He glanced up at Jackson. "On the other hand, Sergeant Major, it might be politic for you to step outside."

Jackson produced a lighter from his pocket and gave him a light. "When you were a subaltern at Caterham, sir," he said with some emphasis, "I had to kick your arse, in a manner of speaking, on a number of occasions. I'm quite willing to do it again if you continue to make suggestions like that."

"My God!" Lopez said. "The bloody English. All mad." He pulled himself toward the box and said to Villiers, "All right, just do exactly as I tell you."

When Elliot finally appeared, coming down the road an hour and a half later, herding the young Argentinian prisoner before him, Korda and Lopez were inside, out of the rain. Villiers, having worked his way down floor by floor, was just finishing disconnecting the final charge.

It was Jackson who went to meet Elliot. "You're late."

"I got a warning bleep. Had to stop to take an emergency signal for you and the major."

Villiers appeared in the doorway. "What's all this about an emergency signal?"

"H.Q. were on the wire, sir. They want to hear from you like yesterday. Sounded real urgent."

It was the throb of the engines that brought Villiers awake with a start. He lay there for a moment in the bunk, staring up at the steel bulkhead, a frown on his face as he tried to remember where he was. And then he remembered—HMS *Clarion,* a conventional submarine, diesel-electric powered, not nuclear. She'd picked them up off Bull Cove that afternoon.

Jackson was sitting in a chair in the corner watching him. "You talk in your sleep, did you know that?"

"That's all I needed. Give me a cigarette."

"I think maybe you've been playing this game too long."

"Haven't we all? Why are we on diesels?"

"Because we're on the surface. Commander Doyle sent me down to tell you to be ready to go in a quarter of an hour."

"Okay, I'll see you up top in five minutes."

Jackson went out and Villiers sat on the edge of the bunk and pulled on the jeans and sweater they'd given him, wondering what this whole business was all about. No one had been prepared to tell him anything, nothing worth knowing anyway.

"Ours not to reason why," he said softly as he pulled on rubber boots and reached for a reefer coat.

The cigarette tasted foul and he stubbed it out. He was tired, that was the trouble. Too damn tired and everything was beginning to blur at the edges. What he needed was a long, long rest.

He went outside and, moving through into the control room, mounted the conning-tower ladder to the bridge. Above him, the round circle of the night was scattered with stars. He breathed salt air in his lungs and felt better.

Doyle was looking toward the shore, night glasses raised to his eyes, Jackson at his side. Villiers said, "How are we doing?"

"There's Uruguay for you. La Paloma a couple of miles to starboard. We're sticking you in as close to Montevideo as possible. Sea's a bit choppy, but it shouldn't give you too much trouble. I suppose you've done this sort of thing rather a lot?"

"Now and then."

Doyle had been watching the shoreline carefully through his night glasses and now he leaned down and spoke briefly into his voice pipe.

The submarine started to slow and Doyle turned to Villiers and said, "As far as we go, I'm afraid. They're bringing your dinghy out of the hatch."

"Thanks for the ride," Villiers said and shook hands.

He went over the side and descended the ladder, Jackson following him, down to the circular hull. The dinghy was already in the water, held by two able seamen. Jackson dropped in and Villiers followed him. There was quite a swell running, and one of the ratings slipped and lost his footing on the slimy steel plates of the hull.

"Ready to go, sir?" the CPO in charge asked.

"No time like the present."

The ratings released the lines, and immediately the tide pulled the dinghy away from the submarine and in toward the shore.

The wind was freshening, lifting the waves into whitecaps. As Villiers reached for an oar, water poured over the side. He adjusted his weight and they started to paddle.

Through the curtain of spray, the shore suddenly seemed very close. Jackson cursed as water slopped steadily over the side, and then they were lifted high on a swell and Villiers saw the wide beach, sand dunes beyond.

The water broke in white foaming spray, they slewed around, and Jackson went over the side, waist deep, to pull them in.

"Ain't life grand?" he said as Villiers stepped out into the shallows.

"Stop grumbling," Villiers told him, "and let's get out of here."

They dragged the dinghy up to the nearest dune, Jackson puncturing it with his knife, and they covered it with sand. Then they walked up through the dunes until they saw a large beach café over on the right, shuttered and dark.

"That looks like it," Villiers said.

There was a dark saloon car parked by the sea wall. As they approached, the door opened and a man in an anorak got out and stood waiting.

"A nice night for a walk, Señors," he said in Spanish.

And Villiers gave the required answer in English. "Sorry, we're strangers here and don't speak the language."

The other smiled and held out his hand. "Jimmy Nelson. Everything went all right then?"

"Soaked to the bloody skin is all," Jackson said.

"Never mind. Get in and I'll take you back to my place."

As they drove away, Villiers said, "Is there any chance of finding out what all this is about?"

"Search me, old boy. I just do as I'm told. Orders from on high and so on. I've got clothes waiting for you, all you need. Full details were supplied as to sizes. Someone was very efficient. Also passports made out in your own names as there seemed no reason why not. Occupation, sales engineer, that holds true for both of you."

"And where do we go?"

"Paris. One snag about that. There's only one direct flight to that fair city and it's on Fridays. However, I've pulled a few strings and got you on an Air France cargo-carrying jumbo that leaves," he glanced at his watch, "around three hours from now, so it's all worked out rather well. You'll be in Paris tomorrow evening, their time. I always get confused about time changes."

"And then what?"

"Search me. I presume Brigadier Ferguson will explain when he sees you."

"Ferguson?" Villiers groaned. "You mean he's behind this?"

"That's right. Anything wrong, old man?"

"Not really, except I'd rather be back behind the lines in the Falklands," Villiers told him.

10

At Charles de Gaulle Airport, Captain George Corwin, Ferguson's man in Paris, was leaning against a pillar, reading a newspaper. It was dark outside, for it was just after nine o'clock. Garcia was standing over by the newsstand trying to look casual and not doing too well at it, when suddenly Raul Montera appeared at the exit from Immigration and Customs. He carried a canvas holdall in one hand and wore jeans and an old leather jacket. Corwin recognized him instantly from the photo supplied by Group Four.

Garcia hurried forward. "A great pleasure to see you, Colonel, and a personal honor for me. Juan Garcia, at your orders."

"At yours," Montera replied politely. "On the other hand, don't you think it might be an excellent idea not to call me colonel?"

"Of course," Garcia said. "So foolish of me." He tried to take the bag from him.

"I can manage," Montera told him, beginning to feel mildly irritated.

"Of course," Garcia said. "This way, then. My car is just outside. I have secured you a fine apartment in the avenue de Neuilly."

Behind them, as they pulled away from the front entrance, George Corwin was already in the back of a black Rover saloon. He tapped the driver on the shoulder.

"Right, Arthur, that green Peugeot estate car. Where it goes, so do we."

The apartment was pleasant enough, very modern and quite luxurious, but no great character. The sort of place that is the same the world over. Its one advantage was the magnificent view of the Bois de Boulogne, just across the road.

"I hope you will find this to your satisfaction, Colonel."

"It's fine," Montera said. "Just fine and, after all, I presume I won't be here very long."

"Señor Donner and Belov, who represents the Russian interest in the affair, would like to see you in the morning at eleven, if that is convenient."

"All right. But then what happens?"

"I've no idea. Señor Donner insists on total secrecy. Perhaps he will be more forthcoming tomorrow."

"Let's hope so." Montera escorted him to the door and opened it. "I'll see you tomorrow then."

He closed the door behind Garcia, turned back to

the sitting room, opened the French window, and moved out on the terrace. Paris, one of his favorite cities and it now very possibly meant Gabrielle.

His stomach hollow with excitement, he went to the phone books, found the one he needed, and leafed through quickly. It was hopeless. There were a large number of Legrands and no hint of a Mademoiselle Gabrielle.

There was London, of course, where she might very well be. The number of the flat in Kensington was burned into his brain. And why not? Even if he didn't speak, he could at least listen to her voice. He checked the area code for London, picked up the phone, and dialed the number. He let it ring for a long time at the other end before putting it down.

There was wine in the refrigerator in the ultra-modern kitchen and sherry. He poured himself a glass of ice-cold Manzanilla and went out and stood on the terrace, sipping it slowly, thinking of her, more alone than he had ever felt in his life before.

"Where are you, Gabrielle?" he whispered aloud. "Come to me. Just a hint."

Sometimes it worked. On the San Carlos run it had saved him more than once, the thought of her, her tangible presence, but not now. Now, there was nothing. He finished his sherry, suddenly tired, went back inside and went to bed.

No more than a mile away on the avenue Victor Hugo, Gabrielle leaned on the rail of the balcony of her own apartment.

There was an unreality to the whole thing. In a way, it was like a dream where things happen in slow motion and one is somehow an observer and not a participant. Somewhere out there was Raul, for Corwin had phoned to warn her that he was expected that night.

The telephone rang in the room behind her and she hurried in and picked it up. Corwin said, "He's here. I followed him and Garcia to an apartment block on the avenue de Neuilly. Just did a bit of judicious bribery and got the number of the apartment. Here's the address."

She wrote it down. "What am I supposed to do? Go round and knock on the door?"

"Not really a good idea," Corwin said. "Let's leave it to Major Villiers, shall we? He'll be arriving tomorrow."

He put down the phone. Gabrielle stood, looking at the address for a moment, committing it to memory, then she tore the paper into pieces, went into the bathroom, and flushed them down the toilet.

"And now the lies begin," she whispered. "And the deceit and the betrayal," and she turned slowly and went back into the sitting room.

The address Belov had given Donner turned out to be a small, back-street nightclub in Montmartre, not far from the Madeleine, run by a man named Gaston Roux.

He was small, with horn-rimmed glasses, and his pin-stripe suit, while of excellent cut, was most conservative. He could have been a lawyer or accountant or even a prosperous businessman, which in a way he was, except that crime—anything from drugs to prostitution—was his business, and his ruthlessness was a byword in the Paris underworld.

"Muscle is what I need," Donner told him as he sipped Roux's excellent cognac. "My contact told me you were just the man to provide it."

"I have a certain reputation, Monsieur," Roux said. "That is true. You need eight men?"

"Right."

"And our mutual friend tells me you would prefer ex-soldiers."

"That's correct."

"So the task would be a formidable one. Can you give me any further information?"

"Not really."

Roux tried again. "Would there be the possibility of a little shooting?"

"Yes, which is why I'm offering twenty-five thousand francs per man."

Roux nodded. "How long would you require them?"

"To sit on their hands in the country for two to three days and receive a certain amount of instruction in what's expected of them. The actual task will take no more than three to four hours in all."

Roux took a deep breath. "Very well. My terms are as follows. One hundred thousand francs for my services as agent, for which I will guarantee you, for thirty thousand francs apiece, eight men who would shoot their grandmothers if you told them to."

"I felt sure I'd come to the right place."

Donner snapped his fingers at Stavrou standing by the door. He came forward, put a dark blue briefcase on the table, and opened it. It was filled with packages of bank notes.

Donner tossed packet after packet across the table. "One hundred and twenty thousand for them, fifty for you. That's half. You get the rest when the job is done."

Roux smiled, showing the glint of gold-capped teeth. "Monsieur, I like you. I really do. In anticipation of a satisfactory conclusion to our business, I have already gathered in a number of suitable specimens. You may take your pick. If you'd like to accompany me, we can settle the matter now."

The sign above the door on a building two streets away said Roux & Sons, Undertakers.

Roux said as he opened the door and led the way in, "A legitimate enterprise. I started it to give a veneer of respectability to certain of my ventures, but my only son, Paul, has really taken it seriously."

"Well, there's no accounting for taste," Donner said.

Roux led the way along a dark corridor lined with waiting chapels. There were actually coffins in some of them, and there was the heavy, cloying scent of flowers on the air.

There was the murmur of voices from behind a closed door at the end of the corridor. Roux opened it and led the way into a large garage containing three hearses and two trucks. There were at least a dozen men waiting, four of them playing cards on the ground, the others simply lounging around smoking and talking.

They were as rough a looking lot as Donner had seen in a long time, most of them old hands from the look of it and around the late thirties or forty in age.

Roux turned. "If you would like to wait outside for a couple of minutes, I'll explain the situation to them." He smiled bleakly. "I always like to achieve a certain understanding with people I engage. Something special between me and them. You understand, Monsieur?"

"But of course," Donner said cheerfully.

He and Stavrou slipped out through a small judas gate into a back yard. Donner took out a cigarette, and Stavrou gave him a light.

"Think you can handle them? They look rough."

"Not if you look twice," Stavrou said.

"We'll see."

Roux opened the door. "Come in, gentlemen."

The men now stood in a line and Donner looked them over. Roux said, "I've explained the situation. Every man here would like to take part. The choice is yours."

Donner simply picked the eight worst looking ones in his own estimation. As he reached the end of the line, tapping each man of his choice on the chest, a large man with a broken nose and close-cropped red hair, one of those left out, said, "Merde!" and spat on Donner's left shoe.

Donner slapped him in the face. The man reeled in shock, then roared with rage and reached out to destroy. Stavrou was somehow in the way. He grabbed for the right wrist, twisted it up and around. The man screamed as muscle tore and, still keeping that terrible hold in position, Stavrou ran him headfirst into a stack of packing cases in one corner. The man fell on his knees, face covered in blood.

"Would anyone care to change his mind?" Donner inquired and nodded at Stavrou. "I should warn you, my friend here will be in charge."

No one moved. In fact, no one said a word, except Roux who sighed heavily and offered Donner a cigarette. "A terrible thing, the corrupting power of money, wouldn't you agree, Monsieur?"

Ferguson had retired to bed early, not to sleep, but to work on more papers in the comfort of his bed. He was just deciding to call it a day when the phone rang. It was Harry Fox.

"Just heard from George Corwin in Paris, sir. Raul Montera turned up on schedule. He was met by Garcia who took him to an apartment in a block on the avenue de Neuilly close to the Bois de Boulogne. He's given Gabrielle the address."

"Good," Ferguson said.

"I'm still worried about her, sir. We're asking a hell of a lot."

"I know. I happen to think she's up to it."

"But dammit all, sir, what you're really requiring

her to do is serve your purposes and destroy herself in the process."

"Perhaps. On the other hand, how many men have died already down there in the South Atlantic, Harry, on both sides? What we've got to do is stop the bloody carnage, or don't you buy that?"

"Of course I do, sir." Fox sounded weary.

"When does Tony get in?"

"About five o'clock tomorrow evening, French time."

"You can take the shuttle over there tomorrow afternoon, Harry. You and Corwin meet him. I want you to fill him in on the whole scene in finest detail."

"He won't like it, sir. Gabrielle's involvement."

"Are you trying to tell me he still loves her?"

"It isn't as simple as that," Fox said. "They were married for five years. All right, a hell of a lot of bad in there, but you can't just toss the relationship out of the window. She's important to him. Let's put it in an old-fashioned way. He still cares for her."

"Excellent. Then he'll make damn sure she doesn't come to any harm. I want you back here tomorrow night, Harry."

"Very well, sir."

"Anything else before I turn out the light?"

""What about the French connection, sir? Isn't it time we brought them in on this?"

"Not really. Certainly not at the moment. We still don't know what Donner is up to. If the French arrested him now, a good lawyer would have him on the street in an hour."

"At least speak to Pierre Guyon, sir."

"I'll think about it, Harry. Go to bed."

Ferguson put down the phone and sat back against the pillows, doing exactly what he had told Fox he'd do—think about it.

The French Security Service, the Service de Documentation Exterieure et de Contre Espionage, the SDECE, is divided into five sections and many departments. The most interesting one is Section Five, more commonly known as the Action Service, the department that had been responsible for destroying the OAS. Colonel Pierre Guyon was in charge of that department, and he was not only Ferguson's opposite number but one of his oldest friends.

Ferguson reached for the phone and dialed the area code for Paris, hesitated, then replaced the receiver. He was taking a chance, he knew that, his entire career on the line. But his instinct, the product of years of experience in intelligence work, told him that he should let things ride and he always trusted his instinct. He switched off the light, turned over, and went to sleep.

Raul Montera slept surprisingly well that night, the strain and fatigue of the past few weeks catching up on him. The result was that he didn't rise until ten o'clock. For years he had been in the habit of running regularly, each morning. The only time he'd had to deviate from his usual practice was during his flying operations out of Rio Gallegos.

He said good morning to Gabrielle, a ritual now, and went to the window. When he drew the curtain and looked out, it was raining hard, the Bois de Boulogne shrouded in mist. He felt suddenly exhilarated. He'd been so tired on the previous evening that he hadn't unpacked his holdall. He did so now, pulled on his old black tracksuit and some running shoes, had a glass of orange juice from the refrigerator, and let himself out.

He liked the rain. It gave him a safe, enclosed feeling, rather like being in a world of your own, and he ran through the park, thoroughly soaked and enjoying every minute of it. He wasn't the only one. There were a number of fellow rain lovers about, some like him, running, others walking the dog, even the odd horseback rider.

George Corwin, hidden in the back of a parked milk van on the avenue de Neuilly, watched Montera running very fast from the direction of the lake. He came to a halt only a few yards away and stood breathing heavily. Corwin took several pictures of him with a special camera through a tiny hole in the side of the van.

As Montera crossed the road, a black Mercedes pulled in at the curb outside the apartment block. Garcia got out, followed by Donner, then Belov.

"Would you look at that now?" Corwin said softly. "Dear old Nikolai himself," and the camera whirred

151

again several times before the three men turned and went into the building.

Stavrou got out of the car to make some sort of adjustment to the windshield wipers and Corwin snapped him too, for good measure.

"Nasty looking bit of work," he murmured.

Stavrou got back in the car. Corwin made himself comfortable, lit a cigarette, and waited.

Raul Montera didn't like Donner one little bit. There was something about the man, something inimical that offended him. Belov he quite liked. A reasonable enough man, working for his own side, which was fair enough, although Montera had never had any great liking for the Communist cause.

He brought a tray in from the kitchen and set it down. "Coffee, gentlemen?"

"Aren't you going to join us, Colonel?" Donner asked.

"I never touch the stuff. Bad for the nerves." Montera went into the kitchen again and returned with a china mug in one hand. "Tea."

Donner laughed and there was an edge to it that indicated that the dislike was mutual. "Rather unusual for a South American, I would have thought."

"Oh, it's surprising what we *dagos* get up to on occasions," Montera told him. "The British Navy would have a useful opinion on that."

Belov said smoothly. "I agree with you, Colonel. A very civilized habit, tea drinking. We Russians have existed on the stuff for years."

Garcia said, "Perhaps we can get down to business. Maybe Señor Donner is now prepared to give us more detail about the operation."

"Of course," Donner said. "I was only waiting for Colonel Montera's arrival. The whole thing, with any kind of luck, should be wrapped up within the next couple of days, which is good because according to the newspapers this morning, the British troops at San Carlos are getting ready to move out."

Montera lit a cigarette. "All right, so what exactly have you arranged?"

Donner had always found, as a matter of policy, that a basis of fact made a phony story sound better.

"As you know, the Libyans have a plentiful supply of Exocets, but due to pressure from the rest of the Arab world, Colonel Qaddafi has not been able to release them to Argentina as he first intended—or perhaps I should say, not officially. There's always a way around most things in this life, or so I've found."

"So?" Montera said.

"I've taken a house in Brittany near the coast, close to an old wartime bomber station. A place called Lancy. Disused now, but the runways are still perfectly usable. Two days from now, possibly three, a Hercules transport en route from Italy to Ireland will put down at Lancy, quite illegally, of course. There will be ten of the latest mark of Exocet missiles on board."

"Holy Mother of God!" Garcia said.

"You, Colonel Montera, will check that cargo. If you're satisfied, you will phone Señor Garcia here in Paris, who will make immediate arrangements to have

153

three million pounds in gold transferred as I direct in Geneva."

"I must congratulate you, Señor," Montera said softly. "That really is the way to wage war."

"I've always thought so," Donner said. "I presume, by the way, that you will want to take off with the Hercules when it leaves, not for Ireland, but for Dakar in Senegal. They're very liberal minded there, especially when it comes to business. The Hercules will refuel, fly across to Rio, where it will refuel again for the final leg of the journey, which will be to any air force base that takes your fancy in Argentina."

There was silence. Garcia said with some awe, "Magnificent."

"And you, colonel?" Donner looked up at Montera. "Do you think it's magnificent?"

"I'm a professional soldier," Montera said. "I don't have opinions. I just do as I'm told. When do you want me at this place?"

"The day after tomorrow. We'll fly down by private plane." Donner stood up. "Until then, enjoy yourself. This is Paris. I'd say you've earned it after your efforts down there in the South Atlantic."

Montera rose and opened the door for them. As they went out. Donner said, "I'll be in touch."

He and the Russian moved down the hall. Garcia lingered a moment. "What do you think?"

"I think I don't like him," Montera said. "But that's not what I'm here for."

"I'd better go," Garcia said. "If anything of importance comes up, I'll phone you. Otherwise, Colonel, you might as well do as Señor Donner suggests—enjoy yourself."

Gabrielle went riding in the Bois de Boulogne at noon. It had stopped raining and there were few people about. She'd slept badly, hadn't risen until just before noon, and hadn't really caught up with herself since. She felt tired and dull and sick with apprehension about the task ahead.

Corwin moved into the shelter of an oak tree as rain began to spot the ground again. He watched Gabrielle canter up through the trees from the direction of the lake, the same route Montera had taken that morning. The ride had brought color back into her cheeks, and she looked quite magnificent.

She reined in as Corwin stepped into view. "Oh, it's you."

She dismounted and Corwin produced a number of prints of the photographs he'd taken that morning and passed them to her.

"Have a look at those. I'll hold the horse."

She looked at the first one. Corwin said, "The small man is Juan Garcia. The big one is Donner and then Belov, the KGB man. Montera, of course, you know."

She stared down at the photograph, her stomach hollow, then glanced at the next one. "That's Yanni Stavrou, Donner's minder. Very rough customer."

And then she came to the ones Corwin had taken

of Montera running in the park, and there was one, where he was at maximum effort, saturated with the pure joy of running, face clear, no pain there at all. She was filled with such love for him that the sensation was almost unbearable. She handed them back and took the reins of the horse.

"Are you all right?" Corwin asked.

"Why shouldn't I be? When does Tony get in?"

"Around five o'clock. Harry Fox will be in before then. The Brigadier wants him to brief your husband thoroughly before he sees you."

"He's not my husband, Mr. Corwin," Gabrielle said and pulled herself up into the saddle. "A very elementary error on your part. People in our game can't afford errors, not even little ones."

She was right, of course, Corwin knew that. Strange that he didn't feel any anger as he watched her canter away.

As Corwin, Jackson, and Tony Villiers went up in the elevator to the tenth floor of the apartment block on the avenue Victor Hugo, Corwin said, "It's quite a reasonable little service flat. I had to take it for a month though, that was the minimum."

"I'm sure the department can stand it," Villiers said.

"Of course, the reason I took it was because Gabrielle lives just up the road. All very convenient." His effort at a smile died in the face of Villiers's implacable hostility.

"I know where she lives, or hadn't that occurred to you?"

He was surprised at the extent of his own anger over such a trivial point. He was tired, that was the trouble, far too tired. Also frustrated and filled with hate when he thought of Charles Ferguson.

The elevator stopped, they got out, and Corwin led the way along the corridor, took out a key, and opened a door. He passed the key to Villiers.

"All yours."

He led the way in and Villiers and Jackson followed. The flat was small, neat, and functional, more like a good modern hotel room than anything else.

Harry Fox sat by the window reading a newspaper. Villiers stood looking at him. "Anything interesting?"

"Not really." Fox put the newspaper down. "The push from San Carlos is expected at any minute."

Villiers tossed his bag onto the bed. "All right, Harry, what's it all about. Last time I saw Ferguson I told him to lay off Gabrielle, so what's his game?"

"You won't like it, Tony."

Villiers said to Jackson, "Get us all a drink, Harvey, I think I'm going to need it." He turned back to Fox. "Okay, let's have it."

At Maison Blanc, the old gypsy, Maurice Gaubert, and his son Paul were setting traps for rabbits in the wood above the house when a truck turned into the stable yard below and braked to a halt. As the Gauberts watched, a number of men got out and a couple who had stayed inside started to pass various items of equipment out. Stavrou got out of the driver's cab and went and unlocked the main stable doors.

Paul Gaubert said, "It's Monsieur Donner's man. The one with the funny name."

"The only funny thing about him," his father said. "Stavrou." He dropped the traps he was holding and picked up his shotgun. "We'll go and see what this is all about."

Stavrou was just coming out of the stables as they approached. He lit a cigarette, leaned against the truck, and waited.

"Bonjour, Monsieur," Maurice Gaubert said. "Rather more of you this time."

"That's right."

"And Monsieur Donner, he comes also?"

"Probably tomorrow."

Paul Gaubert shifted nervously from one foot to the other under Stavrou's grim stare. His father said, "Is there anything you wish us to do, Monsieur?"

"Keep an eye out for any strangers." Stavrou took a couple of thousand franc notes from his wallet and held them up. "You understand me?"

"Perfectly, Monsieur." Gaubert took the money. "Your business is, after all, your own business. If anything unusual occurs, I will let you know."

Stavrou watched them go then turned into the stables where his men were sorting the supplies that had been unloaded from the truck.

"All right, line up," he said. "At the double."

They ran to obey his command and a moment later

stood in line, rigidly at attention. He paced up and down, looking them over.

"As far as I'm concerned, you're back in the army now, so the sooner you get used to that idea, the better."

Corwin had supplied a Citroën rental car and, when it pulled up outside Gabrielle's apartment in the avenue Victor Hugo later that evening, Jackson was at the wheel, Harry Fox and Villiers in the rear.

"So that's it," Fox said. "At least you know the score now."

"So it would seem."

"One other thing. This Professor Bernard I mentioned. They're still phoning him from Buenos Aires for technical information on various aspects of the Exocets they've got left, which can't be many. Our people in B.A. monitored two calls last night."

"That's not so good," Villiers said.

"I know. Brigadier Ferguson feels it can't be allowed to continue. In the circumstances, he'd like you to take care of it while you're here."

"All right," Villiers said without emotion.

"Good. Now if the sergeant major wouldn't mind running me out to Charles de Gaulle Airport, I'll just have time to catch the last shuttle to London."

"All right, Harvey. You take care of Captain Fox," Villiers said. "Don't bother to pick me up. I'll walk back. See you later."

He got out and as he started away Fox half-opened the door. "Tony."

Villiers turned. "What is it?"

"Go easy on her."

Villiers stood there looking at him, face quite blank, hands in pockets, then turned and went into the entrance without another word.

"You're looking well," he said.

She was standing by the fire, gas logs flickering brightly on the hearth. She wore a black silk jumpsuit, her feet bare, hair tied back from the face.

"So are you. What was it like down there?"

"Rather like the Scottish Highlands on a bad day." He laughed harshly. "As far as I'm concerned, the Argentinians can have it. East Falkland has very little to commend it. I'd rather take Armagh or the Oman any day."

"So what's it all about then?" she demanded. "What are we all playing at, Tony?"

Suddenly, there was an intimacy again, a warmth. Not love, not in the strictest sense of the word, but something between them that she knew now would always be there. Would never go away till the day she died.

"Games, my love." Villiers walked to the sideboard and poured himself a brandy. "That's what we're playing at every level from the Prime Minister, Galtieri, and Reagan downward."

"And you, Tony, what kind of game have you been playing all these years? The death-wish game?"

He smiled slightly. "God help me, Gabrielle, but

160

don't you think I haven't looked for an answer to that question a thousand times?"

She frowned as if trying to get it straight in her own mind and sat down. "You see, Tony, in the end, do we control the game or does the game possess us? Can we stop it if we want or must it always be the same?"

He felt a closeness he had not felt before. He sat down opposite, sensing intimacy between them again.

"Montera—you love him, don't you?"

"Yes," she said simply.

"Do you think you can go through with this?"

"I hope so. Ferguson certainly stacked the deck."

"One of these days, I intend to run him down with a rather large truck," he told her. She smiled and he took her hands. "That's better. Now, let's discuss how you and Montera are going to get together again."

"And just how do you intend to arrange that?"

"Simple. Corwin tells me he saw Montera running in the Bois de Boulogne yesterday morning."

"So?"

"He apparently runs extremely well, which would indicate that he's in regular practice, and only fanatics turn out in the pouring rain, the kind who refuse to miss a day's training. My hunch is he'll be there tomorrow."

"And what about me?"

"You can go horseback riding again. Let me explain."

When he was finished she smiled reluctantly. "You always were inventive, Tony."

"In some things." He stood up. "Anyway, I'll be keeping an eye on you. Don't bother to get up. I'll let myself out."

He hesitated and then reached for her hand. She held on tight and when she looked up, her face was tragic.

"I love him, Tony, isn't that the strangest thing? Just like everything I ever read about in the story-books and poetry. Love at first sight. Total possession, so that I can't get him out of my mind."

"I understand."

"And now," she said, clenching her fists, "I'm destroying that love by my actions and I have no damn choice." There was anger as well as tears in her eyes. "I suppose you would say that was rather ironic?"

He had no answer, of course, none at all, only a terrible rage deep inside, against himself and Ferguson and the world they inhabited. He kissed her gently on the forehead, turned, and let himself out quietly.

11

It was raining again the following morning as Gabrielle took the horse forward to the edge of the trees and waited as Villiers had instructed her to. It was very quiet, only the sound of rain hissing through the branches. There was an air of total unreality to everything and she was again conscious of that strange sensation of being an observer watching herself as in a dream.

And then far below, from the trees beside the lake, a figure in a black tracksuit emerged and started to run up the hill. *Raul.* She recognized him instantly, watched for a few moments as she had been told, and then kneed the horse forward.

There was a movement somewhere on her right and two men came out of the trees. One of them was bearded and wore a reefer coat. The other was younger, with long yellow hair, in jeans and a patched denim jacket. And they were trouble, she knew that instantly.

The one with the beard ran forward, flinging up his arms, making the horse rear. As he grabbed for the reins, the other reached up and caught her right arm, and she cried out in genuine fear as she was pulled from the saddle.

They both had her then, the bearded one holding her arms behind her while the boy with the yellow hair moved in close, reaching under her jacket for her breasts.

As the horse cantered away, the bearded one said, "Get her into the trees," and she cried aloud again, not in fear now, but in rage at every man who had ever put a hand on her, and kicked out savagely.

Montera, hearing the first cry, paused and looked up in time to see her come off the horse. He didn't recognize her then, saw only a woman in difficulty, and ran very fast up the slope, his running shoes making no sound on the wet grass.

She was on the ground now, the bearded one trying to pull her up, the other one standing watching. Montera descended like a thunderbolt, delivering a terrible blow to the kidneys, knuckles extended. The boy screamed and fell on his knees. As the bearded man glanced up Montera kicked him in the face.

The soft running shoe didn't do much harm and the man rolled over and came to his feet, pulling a knife from his pocket.

In the same moment, Gabrielle turned, scrambling to her feet, and Montera saw her. He paused, total astonishment on his face, and reached for her instinctively.

She cried a warning as the bearded man rushed in. Montera shoved her away and swayed to one side like a bullfighter, the man stepping past him.

Raul Montera knew a killing rage now, such as he had never known in his life before. He poised, balanced on both feet, waiting, The man rushed in again, knife extended. As it came up, Montera grabbed the wrist, twisting the arm up and to one side, taut as a steel bar. The bearded man screamed, Montera struck him a devastating blow across the side of the neck with the edge of his hand and he went down.

The boy with the yellow hair was being sick and Gabrielle leaned against a tree, her face pale, streaked with mud.

"Gabrielle. Oh my God!" Her name burst out of him and suddenly he was laughing as he held her by the arms and looked at her.

She said shakily. "You don't do things by halves, do you?"

"I could never see the point. In this sort of business, do it properly or run away. I'll get your horse."

It was grazing peacefully nearby, and he caught the reins and brought it over. "Do you want to ride?"

"I don't think so."

The bearded man groaned and tried to sit up. The boy was standing now, leaning against a tree.

"What do you want me to do about these animals? The police?"

"No, let it go," she said. "You've handed out sufficient punishment for one morning."

They started up toward the gates. "This is amazing, truly amazing. I arrived yesterday. I didn't have a Paris address for you, but I did ring the London flat. No answer."

"Obviously not. I'm here." And now it was necessary for her to say the right things. "But what's going on, Raul? You're at war. Why aren't you in Buenos Aires?"

"It's a long story. I'm staying just across the road in avenue de Neuilly. What about you?"

"My apartment is in avenue Victor Hugo."

"Also not too far away," he smiled. "My place or yours?"

The joy in her was so great that for the moment she forgot everything. "Oh, Raul, it's so good to see you."

She reached up and kissed him. He held her for a moment. "Isn't this what the English call serendipity? A spectacularly marvelous, but totally unexpected delight?"

"I believe they do."

There was laughter in his eyes and his mouth was touched by that inimitable smile she knew so well. "I'd say that more than anything else at this particular moment in time you could do with a nice hot bath."

She smiled. "My car is at the stables."

"Then what are we waiting for?"

They went up the slope together, his arm around her, the horse trailing behind them.

* * *

After they'd gone, Tony Villiers and Harvey Jackson moved out of the trees and approached the two assailants. The bearded man was on his feet, clutching his arm, his face twisted with pain. The boy was being sick again.

"I told you to frighten her a little, that's all," Villiers said. "But you tried to be clever. Anything you got, you asked for."

Jackson took several bank notes from his wallet and stuffed them into the bearded man's shirt pocket. "Five thousand francs."

"Not enough," the man said. "He's broken my arm."

"That's your hard luck," Jackson told him in his bad French.

Villiers was angry, face dark, remembering her struggling in their hands, and part of that anger was directed at himself for being responsible.

"We could always break your other arm for you," he said in a low, dangerous voice.

The bearded man swung up an arm defensively. "No, that's it! Enough!"

He turned to the boy, grabbed him by the shoulder with his good hand, and they staggered away.

"Sodding amateurs," Jackson said. "We should have known." But Villiers had already turned away and was walking up the slope toward the road, very fast, head down.

The apartment on avenue Victor Hugo was large and airy, high ceilings, tall windows. The furnishings were simple but very striking, the palest of green curtains, soft and restful, a couple of Impressionist paintings a vivid splash of color against white walls.

Montera sat at one end of an enormous green marble bath sunk into the floor. She came in from the kitchen, quite naked, with two china mugs of tea on a tray. She handed him one, stepped in the other end of the bath, and sat down.

"To us," he said, toasting her.

"To us."

And for the moment, she was able to forget the dreadful situation she was in, was able to think only of the present moment and of the fact that they were together.

He leaned back in the warm water and drank a little tea. "Haven't we done this before somewhere?"

She frowned, running a finger down an ugly half-healed scar six or seven inches long below his right shoulder.

"What happened?"

"Cannon shell splinter. I was lucky that day."

Once again, she had to simulate ignorance. "You mean you've been flying? Flying down there in the Falklands?"

"Malvinas." He grinned. "Always remember that. But yes, I flew a Skyhawk fighter bomber named Gabrielle, featured prominently on television news several times a day."

"You're joking."

"Painted right across the nose of my plane beneath

the cockpit, I assure you. You've been to San Carlos Water and back many times, my love."

Suddenly she remembered the incident in the television department at Harrods, the sound of the commentator's voice, the photos of planes coming in low over San Carlos Water, the missile exploding the Skyhawk, and the people listening who had clapped.

"Yes," he said wryly. "Who would have thought I'd become a television star at my time of life."

She was genuinely angry. "At your age flying a jet plane in action is just plain ridiculous." She touched his face. "Was it really bad, Raul?"

His eyes were haunted, full of pain. "When I left Rio Gallegos, we'd lost approximately half our pilots. Young boys down the drain, Gabrielle. Such waste."

She responded to his pain instinctively. "Tell me about it, Raul. Make me feel it. Get rid of it, my love. Get rid of it."

She reached for his hands and he gripped hers tightly as they sat facing each other. "Remember that uncle of mine, the bullfighter?"

"Yes."

"He used to pray to the Virgin on his knees, just before going into the bullring. Save me from the horns of the beasts, he used to say. I've gone to the horns many times during the past few weeks."

"Why, Raul? Why?"

"Because it's what I do. I fly. It's also what I am, and down there, there was no choice. Could I sit at a desk while those boys went to hell on their own?

You know what we called Falkland Sound? Death Valley."

His eyes were fixed, the skin stretched tightly over the cheekbones. "In the bullring, they have a red door—the door the bulls come through. It's called the Gate of Fear. Death comes through that gate, Gabrielle, a black beast who is dedicated to the idea of killing me. When I flew to San Carlos, the only thing that kept the door closed was you. Once, at one of my worst moments, when she wouldn't respond to the controls, I was getting ready to eject when I swear I smelt that Opium perfume you use. Crazy, perhaps, but it was as if you were with with me."

"What happened?"

All strain went out of him. "I'm here, am I not?" He smiled. "I should have had a photograph in the cockpit and written underneath the words: I'm Gabrielle—Fly me. You can give me one to take back."

"Take back?" She was shocked. "You're not going back down there to fly again?"

He shrugged evasively. "I'll be here for a few days more. I don't know what happens when I return."

"What are you doing here?"

"Business for my government." In a way, he was telling her the truth. "The arms embargo which the French imposed is giving us problems. But enough of that. What about you?"

"I told you I was doing a series for *Paris Match.*"

"While your estimable father supports you in style?"

"Of course."

"Yes. A Dégas on one wall, a Monet on the other in the sitting room."

She slid onto her knees and kissed him on the mouth very, very softly, her tongue savoring him. "I'd forgotten just how gorgeous you are."

"That word again," he mocked her. "Can't you think of something else?"

"Not right now, but take me to bed and I'll try."

Later, lying there in the half light, the curtains partly drawn, she leaned on an elbow and watched him as he slept. His face tightened, there was pain there, he groaned, and suddenly there was sweat on his forehead and he opened his eyes, wide, staring.

She smoothed back the hair from his forehead and kissed him, gently, just like a child. "It's all right. I'm here."

He smiled weakly. "I had the dream again. I've had it so often. Remember, I told you, that time at your flat in London."

"An eagle descending," she said.

"That's right, coming down hard, claws reaching."

"Well, just remember what I told you. Drop your flaps. Eagles overshoot too."

He pulled her close, kissed her neck. "God, you smell good. Warm, womanly—or am I being sexist in saying that? I'm never too sure of my position with you feminists."

"Oh, I'll explain your position in considerable detail." She smiled beautifully and ran a finger down his arm. "I'm Gabrielle—fly me!"

* * *

She came awake again and found him gone. The sensation of panic was terrible. She sat up and glanced at the bedside clock. It was four o'clock. And then he came in, wearing the old black tracksuit and carrying a newspaper.

"I found it in your mailbox."

He sat on the edge of the bed and opened it. "Anything interesting?" she asked.

"Yes, British forces have broken out of the San Carlos bridgehead. Skyhawks attacked the troops on land. Two shot down." He threw down the paper and ran his hands over his face. "Let's go for a walk."

"All right. Give me five minutes."

He waited in the sitting room, smoking a cigarette. When she joined him, she was wearing the jeans and reefer coat he remembered from London.

They went downstairs and got her car and drove to the Bois de Boulogne. Then they simply walked, holding hands, quiet a great deal of the time.

"You're looking better and more relaxed," she said.

"Well, that's you. Some people like drugs, some people like booze, but I'm on Gabrielle, much more efficacious."

She leaned forward and kissed him. "You're such a nice man. Raul. The nicest man I ever knew."

"Ah, well, you make me that way, you see. I told you once before, you make me better."

They walked back toward the parking lot, arm in arm. "What's going to happen to us?" she asked.

"You mean, are my intentions honorable? I thought I made that quite clear in Kensington. I will marry you at the appropriate moment if only to get my hands on the Monet and the Dégas."

"And in the immediate future?"

"A couple of days, if we're lucky, then I must return to Argentina."

She made a determined effort to be cheerful. "So, at least tonight is secure. Let's go somewhere nice where we can dine and dance and be together."

"Where would you suggest?"

"There's a place in Montmartre called Paco's. He's Brazilian. The music is excellent."

"Paco's it is then. I'll pick you up at eight o'clock. Is that okay?"

"Fine."

She glimpsed Tony Villiers by the newstand on the far side of the parking lot, and anger touched her as she unlocked the door of her car. "I'll drop you off at your place."

Which she did, getting out of the Mercedes to stand and talk to him for a moment, before driving away.

On the other side of the road, sitting on a bench reading a newspaper, one of Nikolai Belov's men noted the registration number of the car, got up, and walked away as Montera went into the apartment building.

Back at her apartment, Gabrielle paced up and down, waiting for the ring at the door that she knew must come. When it did, she went and opened it quickly to admit Villiers. She walked back into the sitting room, thoroughly angry, and turned to face him.

"Well?" he said. "Anything to report?"

"He's here on business for his government in connection with the arms embargo."

"That really is a very fair description. Anything else?"

"Yes, I don't want you dogging my heels all the time, Tony. I mean that. This is difficult enough as it is."

"You mean I'm an embarrassment."

"Put it any way you please. I certainly don't need you tonight. We're dining at Paco's in Montmartre."

"And then coming back here?"

She walked over and opened the door. "That's all, Tony."

"Don't worry," he said. "Harvey and I have other fish to fry tonight."

He went out and Gabrielle turned, went into the bathroom, and ran her second bath of the day. She looked forward to the evening with anticipation. Whatever else happened, she was going to have that.

Donner was in the shower when Wanda came in with the hand phone. "Belov wants a word with you."

Donner dried his hands, leaned out, and took the phone. "Nikolai, what can I do for you?" He listened for a while, face inscrutable. "That certainly *is* interesting. Yes, keep me informed. If they go out anywhere tonight, for example, let me know."

He handed the phone back to her. "Trouble?" she said.

"Apparently our war hero has found himself a girl friend. A spectacularly beautiful young woman, according to Belov's information, who lives on the avenue Victor Hugo."

"That usually means money."

"A reasonable deduction. Name of Gabrielle Legrand. Belov's going to keep me informed on the situation. I must say, if she's as good as she sounds, it might be worth taking a look at her."

"You would," she said bitterly and put the hand phone down on a small table by the door. "Do you want anything else?"

"Yes," he said. "You can come and scrub my back."

"If you like."

She started to undress slowly, thinking already with a certain fear of a girl she had never met, some sixth sense telling her she could be in trouble.

Montera had brought only one reasonably formal suit with him. He wore it now, single-breasted, dark blue mohair, with a plain white shirt and black tie.

"You look extremely elegant," she said as they sat together in the back of the cab.

"I pale into insignificance beside you."

She was wearing that spectacular silver mini-dress that she'd worn at their first meeting at the Argentine Embassy in London, the sunburst hair brushed out in *Le Coupe Sauvage*.

"The last time we were out together you introduced

me to the romance of the Embankment at midnight. What have you in store for me tonight, I wonder."

Gabrielle smiled and took his hand. "Nothing very much," she said. "Just me."

Donner was watching the latest news about the Falklands on television when Belov phoned again.

"They've gone out on the town," the Russian said. "A Brazilian restaurant in Montmartre called Paco's."

"Sounds interesting," Donner said. "Is the food any good?"

"Fair, but the music is excellent. The young woman, by the way, is the daughter of an extremely wealthy industrialist named Maurice Legrand."

"What's his line?"

"Just about everything. Operates out of Marseilles. If he went bust, so would the Bank of France."

"Even more interesting," Donner said. "All right, leave it with me." He put down the phone and turned to Wanda, who was reading a magazine by the fire. "Okay, put your glad rags on. We're going dancing."

Belov sat beside the phone at his flat for quite some time after speaking to Donner, a frown on his face. Irana Vronsky brought coffee in from the kitchen on a tray and set it down.

"Something wrong?"

"I don't know. It's this Legrand girl. Something about it doesn't fit."

"What exactly?" she asked as she poured coffee.

"I don't know," he said in considerable irritation. "That's the trouble."

"Then ease your mind in the obvious way," she said as she handed him the coffee. "Run a scale-one check on her."

"An excellent idea. Get started on it first thing in the morning when you go into the office." He sipped some coffee and made a face. "Montera was right. Filthy stuff. Is there any chance of a cup of tea?"

12

Paco's was a great success, full of character and life, tables crowded together, and the five-piece band was sensational. They had a booth to themselves from which they could watch the action. She had a whisky sour and he ordered Perrier water with lime.

She said, "You're still not drinking?"

"I have to stay fit, keep on top of things. Middle-aged man, younger woman. You know how it is?"

"Keep taking the pills," she said. "You're doing all right. Of course, I'm only after your money."

"No," he said. "You've got it wrong. At the present rate of inflation in Argentina, *I'm* after *your* money. Even the Monteras may feel the pinch when this war is over."

But the mention of war brought reality back to her, and that would not do at all. She took his hand. "Come on, let's dance," she said and pulled him to his feet.

The band was playing a bossanova and Montera led her perfectly, dancing extremely well.

As the music finished, Gabrielle said, "That was good. You should have been a gigolo."

"Exactly what my mother used to say. A gentleman shouldn't dance too well." He grinned. "I always adored it. I haunted all the tango bars when I was a boy. The tango, of course, is the only real dance for an Argentinian. It mirrors everything. Political struggles, depressions, life, love—death. You do dance the tango?"

"I've been known to."

He turned to the bandleader and said "Heh, compadre, what about a real tango? Something to move the heart, like 'Cambalache.'"

"Which means the señor is an Argentinian," the bandleader said. "I thought I recognized the accent. A long way from home, especially now, so this is for you and the lady."

He went to the back of the stage and returned with an instrument slightly longer than a concertina. "Ah," Montera said in delight. "We're going to get the real thing. That, my love, is what we call a *bandoneon.*"

"Sounds good," Gabrielle commented.

"Wait and see."

The bandleader started to play, accompanied only by piano and violin. The music touched something deep inside her, for it spoke of the infinite sadness, the longing of love, the knowledge that all that makes life worth living is in the hands of another, to give or withhold.

They danced as one person, together in a way she would never have thought possible. No domination from him, no leading. He danced superbly but also with the most enormous tenderness. And when he smiled, his love was plain, an honest gift, making no demands on her.

It was a performance that fascinated many people, not least Felix Donner, sitting at the bar with Wanda.

"Dear God in heaven," he said. "What a creature. I've never seen anything like her."

Wanda knew the look on his face and in his eye. "Anybody can look good in a dress like that."

"Fuck the dress. She'd look good in anything—or nothing."

As the music faded, several people applauded, but Montera and Gabrielle stayed together for a moment, oblivious.

"You really do love me very much," she said softly, a wonder in her voice.

"I have no choice," he said. "You asked me why I fly. I told you it's what I am. Ask me why I love you. I can only give the same answer. It's what I am."

The feeling of certainty, of serenity that flooded through her, was incredible. She took his hand. "Let's sit down."

At the table, he ordered a bottle of Dom Perignon. "Yes, tango is a way of life in Buenos Aires. I'll take you to San Telmo, the old quarter. The best tango bars in the world. We'll go to El Viejo Almacén. They'll turn you into an expert there in one night."

"When?" she said. "When does all this happen?"

"Well, I'll be damned," Felix Donner said. "Señor Montera. What a pleasant surprise."

He stood there looking down at them, Wanda at his side. Reluctantly, Montera got to his feet.

It was raining when Paul Bernard alighted from the cab on the corner of the street beside the Seine and paid off the driver. It was an area of offices and tall warehouses, busy during the day, but deserted by night. He moved along the pavement, searching for the address Garcia had left for him in the phone message he'd received in his office at the Sorbonne earlier that evening.

He found what he was looking for, a sign over a warehouse that said Lebel & Company, Importers. He tried the small judas gate in the main entrance. It opened to his touch. He slipped through. The warehouse inside was in darkness but there was a light on in the glass-walled office high above.

"Garcia?" he called. "Are you there?"

He saw a shadow behind the frosted glass of the office, the door opened, a voice said, "Up here."

He mounted the rickety wooden steps cheerfully. "I haven't got much time. One of my postgraduate students, a girl of rather interesting proportions, has asked me around to have supper and check her thesis over with her. With any luck it should take me till morning."

He went in through the door and found Tony Villiers sitting at the desk in front of him.

"Who are you?" Bernard demanded. "Where's Garcia?"

"He couldn't make it."

The door closed behind Bernard, and he turned to find Harvey Jackson there. For the first time, he knew a certain fear.

"What's going on here?"

Jackson grabbed him by the shoulders and shoved him into a chair. "Sit down and speak when you're spoken to."

Villiers took a Smith & Wesson from one pocket, a Carswell silencer from another, and screwed it in place. "That means it won't make a sound when I fire it, Professor, but then I'm sure you know that."

"Look, what's all this about?" Bernard demanded.

Villiers laid the Smith & Wesson down on the desk. "It's about the size of your phone bill to the Argentine. Cabbages and kings. Exocet missiles. Oh, and people called Donner."

Bernard was still frightened, but also angry. "Who are you?"

"Until three days ago I was in the Falklands, so I've seen the dead. I'm an officer of the British Special Air Service Regiment."

"Bastard!" Bernard said, his anger overflowing.

"That's it. As someone once rather unfairly put it, we're the nearest thing to the SS the British Army has. I don't know about that. What I do know is that if you don't tell me what I want to know, I'm going to blow your left kneecap off with his." He picked up the Smith & Wesson. "Very nasty trick we picked up from the IRA in Ulster. If that doesn't work, I'll go to work on the right. That should put you on sticks for the rest of your life."

There was a pottery vase with a plant in it on the top shelf at the other end of the room. His hand swung up holding the Smith & Wesson, there was a slight cough, no more than that, and the vase disintegrated.

It was enough. Bernard said, "You know who Donner is?"

"That's right. I also know he's promised to provide several Exocet missiles to Argentine agents in this country within the next few days. Where's he getting them from?"

Bernard said, "He hasn't told me. In fact, to the best of my knowledge, he hasn't told anybody." Villiers raised the gun as if to take deliberate aim and Bernard said hastily, "No, listen to me."

"All right, but you'd better make it good."

"There's a place off the Brittany coast called Île de Roc where they test Exocets. The nearest port is St. Martin. Donner has taken a house near there. I think his intention must be to hijack one of the Aérospatiale trucks as it passes through to St. Martin carrying Exocets for shipment to the island."

His face was haggard, beaded with sweat, and it was obviously the truth as he knew it. Villiers nodded calmly and said to Jackson. "Okay, Harvey. Go and wait for me in the car."

Jackson didn't argue. He went out, closing the door, his footsteps descended the wooden steps. There was silence.

Villiers put the Smith & Wesson on the desk, lit

a cigarette, and stood up, hands in the pockets of his raincoat.

"You don't like the English very much, do you? Why would that be?"

Bernard said, "You ran in 1940 and left us to the Boche. They shot my father, burned our village. My mother . . . " He shrugged, the despair of years on his shoulders.

Villiers turned and walked to the other end of the office and examined the notice board. Bernard looked across at the Smith & Wesson on the other side of the desk nervously.

"My father was in S.O.E. during the war," Villiers said. "The French section. Dropped into France by parachute three times to work with the Resistance. Finally, he was betrayed, arrested and hauled off to Gestapo headquarters in the rue des Saussaies in Paris. A good address for a bad place. He was interrogated for three days with such brutality that to this day his right foot is still badly crippled."

He turned, hands still in the pockets of the raincoat, and found Bernard still sitting, but now clutching the Smith & Wesson.

"Oh, but you must let me finish, Professor. I've saved the best to last. His torturer was a Frenchman in the pay of the Gestapo. One of those fascists you find everywhere."

Bernard cried something unintelligible and fired. Villiers was already dropping to one knee, his hand emerging from the front of the raincoat holding a

Walther PPK. He shot Bernard in the center of the forehead, hurling him backward, still seated in the chair.

Villiers retrieved the Smith & Wesson, switched off the light, and went out. He descended the stairs, crossed to the judas gate, and stepped into the night. Car lights turned on farther up the street and the Citroën slid into the curb, Jackson at the wheel. Villiers got into the passenger seat.

"Did you give him a chance?" Jackson asked.

"Of course."

"I can imagine. Why not just shoot the poor sod in the first place and get it over with? Why pretend? Did it make you feel better? Every man deserves a chance to draw, just like a fucking western?"

"Just drive, Sergeant Major," Villiers said and lit another cigarette.

"Deepest apologies," Jackson told him. "I trust the major will forgive me. I was forgetting he was a moralist."

He moved into gear and drove away.

Donner ordered another bottle of champagne. "You're not drinking," he said to Montera and tried to fill his glass.

Montera put his hand in the way. "No, thanks. Champagne doesn't agree with me."

"Nonsense," Donner said. "A man who is tired of champagne is tired of life, wouldn't you agree, Mademoiselle Legrand?"

"Actually, a nonsensical proposition. No substance to it at all," she said.

He laughed. "That, I like. A woman who says what she thinks. Just comes right out with it. Now Wanda here, she never says what she thinks. What she tells you is what she believes you'd like to hear, isn't that so, Wanda?"

The young woman's discomfort was plain. Her hands clutched her sequined evening purse tightly. Gabrielle opened her mouth to speak, her anger evident. Raul put a hand on hers and leaned across the table.

"Please, Miss Jones, it would give me the greatest of pleasure to show you how we dance the tango in Argentina."

There was astonishment on her face for a moment, then she glanced at Donner. He ignored her and poured more champagne into his glass. She made her decision and stood up.

"I think I'd like that," she said and walked on to the floor.

"I shan't be long," Montera said to Gabrielle and smiled. "If he annoys you, this one, let me know and I'll give him what the bearded one got."

"Do you possibly think you could guarantee that?"

He leaned over, kissed her as if Donner wasn't there, and joined Wanda on the floor.

"Very nice," Donner said. "I like a good show. Do I get to dance, too?"

Gabrielle sipped a little champagne. "I couldn't

imagine any circumstance in which I would agree to dance with you, Mr. Donner. You see, it's really very simple. I don't like you."

Donner's anger showed only in his eyes, the rest he managed to control. "I'm very persistent. I could grow on you."

"Men." She shook her head. "The arrogance of you. That stupid male arrogance. Selfish, demanding. You treat women with contempt, you know that? Your interest is actually an insult."

He managed to stay good humored on the surface. "I see, so it's men you don't like, not just me? Where does that leave our gallant colonel? He's different, I suppose?"

"He's himself. He doesn't take, he gives." It was as if she were saying this to make sense of it to herself, and there was a kind of joy on her face. "Which may seem a contradiction to you but makes perfect sense to me."

Before Donner could reply the headwaiter appeared at his side. "Monsieur Donner?"

"That's right."

"You left your name at the bar in case there was a phone call. Someone is on the line now."

Donner followed him across to the reception desk and picked up the phone. "Donner here."

"Nikolai. Listen, Garcia's been in touch. Apparently Bernard left him a note earlier this afternoon giving details of convoys to St. Martin for Île de Roc during the next four days. Only one meets your requirements. It will be in the right vicinity very easily on the morning of the twenty-ninth."

"That's the day after tomorrow."

"Correct. Can you handle it?"

"No problem. We'll fly down in the Chieftain in the morning. I'll take the colonel with me."

"Excellent. How did you find the Legrand woman?"

"Very impressive indeed. I might suggest that she come down with us."

"Do you think she will?"

"Maybe. They're obviously crazy about each other."

"Actually, it's not such a bad idea," Belov said.

"Why?"

"I don't know. There's something about her that doesn't quite fit. One gets an instinct for these things."

"You better check her out thoroughly then."

"Oh I will. I'll be in touch tomorrow. Call you at Maison Blanc."

Donner put down the phone and took his time over lighting a cigarette, looking across at Gabrielle, thinking about what Belov had said. God, but she was beautiful, but it was so much more than that. He had been content to use women carelessly all his life, had never experienced any great difficulties with them until now. He shook his head in a kind of reluctant admiration and realized, with some surprise, that he had never wanted a woman so much.

On the dance floor, Wanda glanced across at him, saw the expression on his face, and said to Montera, "She means a lot to you, that lady?"

"Everything," he said simply.

"Then watch him," she said. "He's used to getting what he wants."

As the music finished, he smiled and kissed her hand. "You're too good for him."

She smiled sadly. "You're wrong. I'm no good for anything else."

As they reached the table, Donner joined them. "I've just had a phone call," he said to Montera. "That business transaction of ours takes place Saturday. It means we'll have to fly down to Lancy in the morning. I've taken an old house in the country, Maison Blanc. Very relaxing."

Montera's heart sank. "If you say so."

Donner turned to Gabrielle. "How would you feel about a couple of days in the country?"

"I don't think so," she said, and then saw the look on Montera's face and realized how little time would be left to them now. For the moment it drove all consideration about her mission for Ferguson entirely out of her mind.

"Sleep on it," Donner said.

She stood up. "And now, if you'll excuse us. I'm very tired."

"Of course," Donner said.

He watched them go, frowning slightly, paused to pay the bill, then walked out without a word to Wanda, who hurried after him, desperately unsure of her balance on the ultrahigh heels she wore.

He was on the pavement waiting for a taxi, lighting

a cigarette, the match flaring in his cupped hands, when she caught up with him.

He said, without looking at her, "You made me look a fool in there, you know that?"

"I'm sorry, Felix."

"I'll think of something good," he said. "Very special. The kind of thing you won't forget in a hurry." He pushed her chin up with the tips of his fingers. "Give *you* something to think about, won't it?"

Back at her apartment, Gabrielle mixed herself a whisky sour and paced up and down angrily.

"That man is the most disgusting object I have ever encountered. Everything I hate. Do you have to do business with him?"

"I'm afraid so, but forget him," Montera said. "I've got something for you." He took a small package from his pocket. "After you left me this afternoon, I called a cab and went shopping."

The elegant wrapper said Cartier. She opened it without a word and took out a velvet-covered box. Inside was a beautiful ring, or rather three rings, intertwined in different shades of gold.

"It's what they call a Russian wedding ring," he told her. "Usually worn on the little finger of the left hand."

"I know," she said.

"I had to make an informed guess about the size. If it's wrong, simply call at Cartier's any time you like and ask for a Monsieur Bresson. He'll see to it for you. May I put it on?"

She held out her hand and he slipped on the ring. "I think it may be just a little slack."

She shook her head, staring down at it. "No," she said in a low voice. "It's perfect."

"A token," he said. "Of . . . " He hesitated and grinned crookedly. "My big moment and I can't find the words."

She put a hand on his arm. "Raul, do something for me."

"Anything."

"Go for a walk. I'd like to be alone for a little while."

He was full of concern. "I'm sorry. I'll go back to my apartment. Perhaps I can see you in the morning before I leave."

"No." Her voice rose in a kind of panic. "I want you to come back."

"Of course, my love." He kissed her gently. "Half an hour," and went and let himself out.

"Gabrielle," she said when Villiers picked up the phone.

"Anything for me?"

She took a deep breath and said, "Donner joined us tonight. I heard him tell Raul that the transaction was to take place on Saturday morning and that it would be necessary to fly to Lancy in the morning. I don't know where that is."

"Brittany," he said. "It fits in with facts we already know."

"He suggested I fly down with them. The house they're staying at is called Maison Blanc."

"And you said yes?"

"I want out, Tony. I can't take any more."

"I know it's hard," he said. "But it has to be done. I know what you think of Montera. As a man, I admire him totally, but he is the enemy, Gabrielle, and we're not talking about personalities. We're talking about stopping Exocets."

"It's no good," she said.

"All right. I'm not going to twist your arm. I'll try and handle it without you. But you'll have to tell Ferguson. Check with me in the morning, in case you change your mind."

He put down the receiver, picked it up again, and dialed the number of the Cavendish Square flat in London. It was Harry Fox who answered the phone.

"Bad news from the front," Villiers told him. "Gabrielle, just been in touch. Things are working well, but she feels she can't keep it up. She wants out."

"All right," Fox said. "Leave it with me."

Gabrielle poured herself another drink and sipped a little to steady her nerves, but it had to be done. She sat down and dialed Ferguson's number in London. He answered the phone himself almost instantly.

"Ferguson."

"Gabrielle."

193

His voice changed. "My dear girl, have you been out? I tried to ring you several times earlier."

"Yes, to dinner," she said.

There was a pause, and she was filled with a sudden foreboding.

"Look, this isn't easy," he said. "We tried to reach your mother and stepfather but it seems they're on a yacht cruising the Greek Islands."

It could only be one thing, of course. "Richard?" she whispered.

"Yes, my dear. I'm terribly sorry to have to pass you such news. He's reported missing, believed killed, in flying operations near Port Stanley."

"Oh, God." As Ferguson talked on she sat there remembering how close she and Richard were as children. Her mother and stepfather traveled often and she and Richard were always together. They aligned themselves against the various nannies and servants left to supervise them. And when Richard started going on dates it was Gabrielle who would give him advice. She couldn't believe she'd never see him again . . .

"Naturally, I realize the effect this unfortunate business will have on you," Ferguson said. "In the circumstances it would probably be better to pull you out."

"No," she said wearily. "No point in that. Not now. Thank you and goodnight, Brigadier."

She sat there staring at the phone, then picked it up and dialed Villiers' number again.

"I've changed my mind, Tony. I'll fly down with Raul and Donner tomorrow to this place Lancy. I can't give you the address of Donner's house there though."

"No problem," he said. "Harvey and I will drive down overnight. We'll find it." He hesitated. "Is anything wrong? What made you change your mind?"

"Richard's gone," she said. "Killed in action. It's got to stop, Tony, for everyone's sake. Too many dead already."

"Oh, my God," Villiers said and she put down the phone.

Ferguson sighed. "A remarkable girl."

Harry Fox said, "She won't pull out?"

"No."

"How did she take it?"

"How the hell do I know, Harry. The important thing is how long she can hold herself together."

When Montera reached the door, it was standing slightly ajar, waiting for him. He closed it and went into the sitting room.

"Gabrielle?"

"In here."

She was lying in bed in the darkness. He reached for the switch and she said quickly. "No, Raul, don't turn on the light."

He sat on the edge of the bed and there was concern

in his voice. "Look, my love, if you're not well, I can go. No trouble."

"No." She reached for him. "Don't leave me. I want you here in bed with me."

He undressed, dropping his clothes on a chair, and slipped in beside her. She turned into him, arms sliding about his neck and suddenly, like a dam bursting, all the pain, all the anguish, flowed out of her and she started to cry, slow, bitter tears.

"What is it?" he asked.

"Nothing, Raul. Don't say anything. Just hold me."

He soothed her then, his lips on her forehead, as one might soothe a child, and after a while, she slept.

13

Villiers and Jackson had driven down from Paris overnight, through Orléans and Tours to Nantes, where they had turned south. It was still early, only eight o'clock, when they finally found Lancy. Jackson slowed the Citroën as they came to the perimeter fence. He coasted along past the main gate, which was padlocked, and then picked up speed and drove on, turning into some trees around a bend in the road.

They walked back through the trees and looked down at the airfield. "Old wartime station from the look of things," Villiers said.

"And no sign of life." Jackson shivered. "I hate places like that. Too many ghosts. Too many good men gone."

Villiers nodded. "I know what you mean." He looked up at the gray sky, which threatened rain. "Let's hope the weather doesn't give our friends problems getting in."

Jackson said, "What do we do now?"

"We'll go into this place St. Martin. See if we can find where Donner's house is."

They turned and went back through the trees.

Gabrielle lay on her back, staring up at the ceiling. After a while, she turned her head and found Montera watching her.

"How are you this morning?" he asked gravely.

"Fine." Amazing how calm she felt, how much in control. "I'm sorry about last night."

He reached for one of her hands and kissed it. "Do you want to tell me about it?"

"Nothing to tell," she said. "Old ghosts, that's all." She held his hand tightly. "This business with Donner in Brittany. It's important?"

"Yes," he said.

"And when it's completed, you'll return to Argentina? How long, Raul? Two days? Three?"

"I don't have any choice," he said simply.

"And neither do I. I must take what time there is, even if I have to share you with bloody Donner. I'm coming with you to Lancy."

The delight in his face was plain. "You're sure?"

"Very."

She rolled over, and he buried his face in her neck. She stroked his hair and stared up at the ceiling again. Amazing how easily they came, the lies, the deceit.

* * *

At Brie Comte Robert, Donner walked up and down impatiently, smoking a cigarette. Wanda leaned against the hangar wall, Rabier waited beside the Chieftain.

"Where the hell is he?" Donner demanded, and then a cab turned in through the main gate and crossed the apron toward them.

Raul Montera got out wearing jeans and his old black flying jacket. He turned and held out a hand to Gabrielle. Donner was delighted, all anger leaving him as he went to meet them.

"So, you decided to join us after all?"

"Yes," she said simply. "On reflection, I decided I'd nothing better to do."

Behind her, Montera was getting the bags and paying off the driver. Amazing how marvelous she looked in jeans and the blue reefer coat. Donner had never felt like this in his life before, and it occurred to him with a kind of wonder that this was different. He wanted this woman to want him.

"Fine," he told her. "Let's get moving then."

They turned and walked toward the Chieftain. Wanda came forward and glanced at Montera, that look on her face again.

He smiled. "You worry too much."

"And maybe you should worry more," she said and followed the others.

The small bar on the quay at St. Martin was empty except for Villiers and Jackson, who stood at one end eating the croissants the owner, a large, matronly blonde, had served them.

"More coffee?" she asked.

Villiers nodded. "Where are all the customers?"

"The regulars are working, Monsieur, and we don't get many tourists these days. Things aren't as they were."

"I thought there was an airfield near here?"

"Ah, yes, at Lancy, but that closed down years ago." She poured hot coffee. "You gentlemen have business here?"

"No," Villiers said. "We've been touring Brittany by car for the past week. Someone told us the sea fishing was good here."

"That's true. Best on the coast."

"Where could we stay?"

"Well, there's the hotel up the street, the Pomme d'Or, but not if you take my advice. It's a dump. Hugo, the real estate agent, has plenty of places to rent. Bungalows, cottages, and that sort of thing. He'd be only too pleased to see you, believe me. As I say, we don't get the tourists these days like we used to. His office is only fifty yards along the front."

"I'm very grateful." Villiers delivered his most charming smile. "We'll call on him now."

Monsieur Hugo, a kindly, white-haired old man who appeared to run his office singlehanded, was most accommodating. He had a large map of the area on the wall, little red flags on pins indicating the location of his properties.

"I could find you something here in town with no difficulty," he said. "Of course the minimum period would be one week."

"No problem," Villiers said. "However, I would prefer something in the country. A friend in Paris who stayed here some years ago mentioned a house called Maison Blanc."

The old man nodded, took off his glasses, and pointed to one of the flags. "Ah yes, a fine house, but much too large for your purposes, and in any case, I only recently leased it to a gentleman from Paris."

"I see." Villiers examined the map and pointed to one of the flags situated between Maison Blanc and Lancy. "What about that?"

"Yes. I'm sure that would meet your requirements perfectly. A small modern bungalow called Whispering Winds built five years ago by a schoolmaster in Nantes for his retirement. He only uses it for vacations at the moment. Fully furnished, two bedrooms. I could let you have that for five hundred francs for the week, plus a hundred-franc deposit against breakages. In advance, of course." He smiled apologetically. "It is a sad fact of life, Monsieur, but I'm afraid it has been my experience in the past that there are those who leave without paying."

"I perfectly understand." Villiers took out his wallet and counted the money out on the desk.

"Would you like me to take you out and show you the place?" the old man asked.

"Not necessary. I'm sure you have work to do. If you'll just give me the key."

"Of course, Monsieur." The old man took it from a board and handed it to him. "There is an excellent general store down the street. I'm sure Madame Dubois can meet all your requirements."

Villiers went out to the Citroën and got in. Harvey Jackson said, "Okay?"

"You could say that. I found out where Maison Blanc is and I've got us a holiday bungalow nearby." He held up the key. "Whispering Winds."

"God Almighty," Jackson said.

"Stop off at the store up the street. We'll need a few things."

Villiers sat back and lit a cigarette. It was all going rather well. Now, all that was needed was Donner and Raul Montera and Gabrielle, and the game could begin.

When the Chieftain touched down at Lancy just before noon, Stavrou was waiting to meet it with a large Peugeot estate car. Villiers, watching from the trees on the hill through field glasses, saw the passengers get out of the plane, which then taxied inside one of the hangars, the doors of which Stavrou had opened earlier. He helped Rabier close them and the others got into the Peugeot.

"Gabrielle there?" Jackson asked.

Villiers nodded as Rabier got into the front seat beside Stavrou and the Peugeot drove away.

"Okay, let's get back to the bungalow and have something to eat, and I'll phone the Brigadier. Give our friends a chance to settle down. We can check out Maison Blanc later."

They turned and went back to the car.

Harry Fox was having an early lunch when there was a collect call from Villiers. He said, "He's not here, Tony. Attending a meeting of the Joint Chiefs at the Ministry of Defense. I expect him back within the hour. Where are you?"

"The depths of the Breton countryside. A holiday cottage called, if you would believe it, Whispering Winds."

"And Donner?"

"Just up the road."

"Fine. Give me your number and I'll call the moment he gets back."

At Maison Blanc, Donner opened the door of one of the bedrooms on the first floor and ushered Montera and Gabrielle in. It was an old-fashioned room with a high ceiling and tall narrow windows, rather somber because of the wine-colored wallpaper. There was an old-fashioned bed, very high off the floor.

"Bathroom through there," Donner said. "All the comforts. Stravrou tells me lunch in half an hour. I'll see you down there."

He went out and Montera sat on the bed and bounced up and down. "Mother of God, listen to those springs. The whole world will know of my mad passion for you."

She sat on the bed beside him. "I don't like this place, Raul, and I don't like him."

"I know," he said. "But you like me, so that's all right."

He turned her head and kissed her gently.

Villiers was having a drink in the sitting room, waiting for Ferguson's call, when Jackson came in from the kitchen.

"I was just listening to the radio from Paris. There was a news flash. Apparently 2 Para hit Goose Green early this morning."

"What's the score?"

"Apparently very heavy fighting, according to American sources."

Villiers kicked a chair. "And here we are, playing games for schoolboys."

"Don't be stupid," Jackson said flatly. "They're damned important games. I've opened a can of soup and there's French bread and cheese. If you want some, come into the kitchen. If you want to stay in the officers' mess, that's up to you."

He went out, and at that moment the phone rang. Ferguson said, "How are things, Tony?"

"Moving quite well." Villiers explained in detail. When he was finished, Ferguson said, "Good, the moment you have details of Donner's actual intentions, phone me instantly, and I think you'd better leave Sergeant Major Jackson by the phone at your end in case I need you in a hurry."

"All right, sir," Villiers said. "We just heard a news flash here about the battle at Goose Green."

"Good God," Ferguson said. "It's not even been announced here yet."

"What's happening?"

"Very heavy going, Tony. The truth is our intelligence was faulty. A lot more Argentines there than we thought. I'm afraid the C.O. has been killed, but information is thin on the ground at the moment. Anyway, I'll be in touch."

Villiers put the phone down, his face grim, then he went into the kitchen slowly.

Lunch consisted of vast helpings of smoked salmon and Beluga caviar with Krug champagne to wash it down.

"I'm on a diet," Donner explained. "So if I suffer, my guests suffer. You're not drinking again, Colonel?"

"As I told you, champagne doesn't agree with me."

"What would you like then? A good host should always try to please even the most difficult of his guests."

Montera looked across at Gabrielle who smiled, knowing what he would say. He smiled right back at her. "How about a nice cup of tea?"

"Dear God," Donner groaned and looked up at Stavrou standing by the door. "See what you can do."

Stavrou went out, and Montera said, "We really must have a talk, Donner. Settle our business. When you can find time, that is."

"No time like the present," Donner turned to Gabrielle and Wanda. "Would you ladies excuse us for a while?"

"No problem," Gabrielle said. "I'll go for a walk." She glanced at Wanda. "What about you, Miss Jones?"

Donner laughed. "Wanda, go for a walk? That'll be the day."

The girl colored and stood up. "Thanks very much, but I think I'll unpack."

She went out and Donner said to Gabrielle, "Just one point. The stable is out of bounds for sound business reasons." He smiled. "Anywhere else, feel free."

She opened the French windows and moved out.

Donner and Montera sat by a log fire in the sitting room. Montera said, "You really can guarantee there will be no slip-ups?"

"Absolutely not. My Italian agents assured me this morning that everything is set and ready to go. Those Exocets will be here tomorrow morning without fail. I hope your gold is just as available in Geneva."

"No problem there, I can assure you."

Donner lit a cigarette. "So, you'll fly off in the Hercules. What about Mademoiselle Legrand? Does she go with you?"

"Very probably," Montera said. "If I can persuade her." He stood up. "I think I'll take a walk myself."

"I'll come with you," Donner told him. "I could do with some fresh air."

There was really nothing Montera could say, so they went out together.

Tony Villiers, hidden in the undergrowth behind a wall high above the estate, had noticed several interesting things. Stavrou, for example, crossing from the rear of the house to the stables on occasion. There was someone in there, a face barely glimpsed when the door was opened.

And then Gabrielle appeared, crossing the terrace and starting across the lawn into the trees. He followed her with his field glasses, losing her once or twice. She finally emerged by a small lake and followed a path around it toward a ruined summerhouse on the other side.

And then Villiers's practiced eye detected a movement in the trees above the lake. He focused his glasses and a figure in patched jeans, long hair hanging beneath a tweed cap, a shotgun under his arm emerged from the bushes. He went after Gabrielle, keeping out of sight. Villiers got to his feet and ran down through the trees.

Gabrielle pushed open the broken door of the summerhouse and stepped inside. There was a wooden table, a couple of chairs, a stone fireplace. Various panes of glass were missing in the windows, the floor was damp where rain had drifted in. There was a step behind her and she turned.

The young man who stood there was of medium height with a weak sullen face. He badly needed a shave. His clothes were too large for him, and his hair poked untidily from beneath the cap. He held a double-barreled shotgun in both hands.

"What do you want?" she said.

He ran a hand across his mouth, his eyes glittering as they looked her over. "Oh, no. That's what I ask you. I'm supposed to guard this estate."

"I see." She leaned back on the table. "What's your name?"

He grinned. "That's more friendly. It's Paul. Paul Gaubert."

She brushed past him and went outside. "Heh, come here," he called, ran after her, and caught her by the right arm.

She said, "Don't be stupid. I'm a guest of Monsieur Donner's."

She pulled her arm free and sent him away with a vigorous shove of both hands. He staggered back for a moment and gaped in astonishment. Suddenly, there was only anger there. He dropped the shotgun and grabbed at her, and she put her knee into his groin.

Donner and Montera came over the top of the small hill above the lake in time to witness the whole scene, including the timely arrival of Villiers, although at that distance they could not see the cold fury in his eyes as one hand fastened on Paul Gaubert's collar, the other on his belt. Villiers turned him around and ran him headfirst into the lake. The boy went under, came up, gasping, out of the shallows and up the bank.

"Gaubert!" Donner cried as he ran down the hill with Montera.

The youth glanced over his shoulder, a look of terror on his face, and took to his heels.

Villiers said to Gabrielle. "Are you all right?"

"Fine," she said. "But could we change the script? This sort of thing's beginning to get a trifle monotonous and watch yourself, we ve got company."

"I'm an Irishman on holiday staying at a bungalow not far from here. Michael O'Hagan."

The Irish situation had forced the SAS to develop a language laboratory system of teaching regional Irish accents to their men. Villiers could sound as if he'd been born and bred within five miles of Crossmaglen if he wanted to, and Michael O'Hagan was an alias he had used before.

Montera arrived on the run, full of concern. "Gabrielle, are you all right?"

"Yes, thanks to this gentleman."

"O'Hagan," Villiers said cheerfully in English. "Michael O'Hagen."

"I want to thank you, sir." Donner took his hand. "Felix Donner. This is my place, by the way, and this is Mr. Montera and the lady you rescued is Miss Legrand. The creature who attacked Miss Legrand is a gypsy called Gaubert. I allowed a band of them to stay on the estate, which shows what happens when you treat people like that as human beings."

"Happy to know you," Villiers said.

"Just where did you come from exactly, Mr. O'Hagan?"

"Just up there where the trees flank the road." Villiers pointed. "I was looking at the map, trying to get my bearings, when I saw that character obviously trailing Miss Legrand."

"You're staying near here?"

There was little point in trying to pretend otherwise. Villiers said, "At a little bungalow up the road with a friend. We're on a motoring tour of Brittany."

He had tried to sound simple, open, and ingenuous and appeared to have succeeded. Donner said, "Come back and have a drink with us."

Villiers said, "That's very nice of you, but perhaps some other time. I'm already later than I said I would be."

Donner persisted. "Join us for dinner tonight, then. Bring your friend."

"I don't really have any decent clothes with me," Villiers said, keeping up the image.

"Doesn't matter. All totally informal. Bring your friend."

"All right. I can't speak for him though. He might have other plans."

"Seven-thirty for eight."

Villiers turned and walked briskly away. Montera said, "Lucky he was around."

"Yes, wasn't it?" Donner said, frowning slightly.

At the bungalow, Villiers shaved and had a shower. When he went into the kitchen he was wearing jeans, a dark shirt, and a tweed jacket. He had a Walther PPK in one hand and a roll of surgical tape in the other. He put his left foot on a chair, pulled up his trouser leg and taped the weapon just above the ankle.

"Daniel in the lion's den?" Jackson commented.

"Well, you never know. Comforting to have an ace in the hole. I'll see you later. Be good."

He went out and got into the Citroën and drove away. Jackson poured himself another cup of coffee and reached over to switch on the radio. There was a sudden cool breeze on the back of his neck as if a door had opened. He turned quickly as Yanni Stavrou stepped in, a gun in one hand, two of Roux's recruits standing behind him.

Beyond the French windows the beech trees above the lawn were cut out of black cardboard against a sky that was touched with streaks of orange among the scudding clouds. Inside it was warm and comfortable.

Gabrielle wore her yellow jumpsuit, Montera jeans and a blue flannel shirt. Donner's concession to informality was to wear a mohair pullover instead of a jacket.

He glanced out of the French windows before closing it. "We could have weather trouble soon."

"Don't be a pessimist," Montera told him. "That was an excellent dinner, by the way."

"That's Wanda's department, not mine. She does all right when she tries."

The condescension was plain. Gabrielle said, "It

was more than all right. It was superb. I'd say she has real flair."

"Don't tell her that, for God's sake. She won't be fit to live with."

Wanda entered at that moment with a tray. She was the most dressed-up person there and wore a two-piece evening pants suit in black velvet.

She'd brought tea for Montera and Gabrielle. Donner said, "You are trying, aren't you, but what about Mr. O'Hagan here? All Irishmen drink tea, isn't that true, O'Hagan?"

"Oh, I don't know," Villiers said brightly. "I like a cup of coffee myself."

The girl's hand was shaking as she passed him the cup, and Gabrielle, angry again, turned to Montera. "I feel like a little air. Shall we take a walk?"

"Why not?"

He opened a French window and they went out. Donner said, "A handsome couple, wouldn't you say?"

Villiers managed to look mildly surprised. "Yes, I suppose so."

"Tell me, what do you do for a living, Mr. O'Hagan?"

"I'm a sales engineer. Oil pumps, mainly."

"That must be a good line these days what with North Sea oil."

"Oh, yes." Villiers glanced at his watch. "It's really been wonderful, but I'm afraid I'll have to be going. We have an early start tomorrow."

"What a shame. Still, it's been nice having you."

Donner walked through to the front door with him and opened it. "I'd like to thank you again for what you did. I sent my man Stavrou along to sort that gypsy out earlier this evening, but by the time he'd reached the encampment, they'd all cleared off."

They shook hands and Villiers went down the steps. Donner went back to the sitting room.

Wanda said, "Can I get you anything?"

"No," he said. "Go to bed."

"But it's early, Felix."

He shook his head. "You never learn, do you?" He ran the back of his hand down her face and she shrank back as if expecting a blow. "That's right," he said. "Do as you're told and go to bed."

Stavrou came into the room as Wanda went out. Donner said, "Is the car ready?"

"Yes."

Donner went to the open French window. He could see the glowing end of Montera's cigarette on the other side of the lawn where he and Gabrielle talked.

"Heh, you two. I've got to go out for a little while. Help yourself to drinks, okay?" He turned back into the room and said to Stavrou, "All right, let's get moving," and led the way out quickly.

Montera smoked his cigarette and leaned on the balustrade beside her. "I seem to have done nothing but talk about my mother and my daughter. You must be quite bored."

"I want to know these things, Raul."

"Yes," he said. "Life is nothing without roots, that's

213

true, isn't it? We all need a place to rest our heads from time to time. A place where we can be certain of perfect understanding."

"I wish to God there was such a place for me," she said, and there was a poignancy in her voice that went straight to his heart.

He said, "But there is, my love. Tomorrow I fly back to Argentina direct from here."

"But I don't understand."

"From Lancy. There's a plane putting down with war supplies. A Hercules transport. You could come with me."

And she could, that was the truth of it. It would be so easy. At that moment, she was closer to telling him the truth than she had ever been.

When Villiers went in the front door of the bungalow he called, "Hey, Harvey, where are you?"

There was no reply, but a radio sounded faintly and rather eerily from somewhere at the back of the house. Strangely enough he recognized the song. A nostalgic record. Al Bowlly, the famous crooner of the thirties, singing "Moonlight on the Highway."

The bedroom door stood ajar and Villiers paused on the threshold. Jackson sat at a table on the opposite side of the bed, a small radio playing beside him.

"Hey, Harvey," Villiers said. "What in the hell are you up to?"

And then he moved close enough to see that Jackson was tied to the chair. His cheeks were badly blistered, probably from repeated applications of a cigarette lighter flame. There was a bullet wound just above his right ear, small caliber, as there was no exit wound, and the sightless eyes stared into the wall.

Villiers slumped down on the bed and simply sat there looking at him. Aden, the Oman, Borneo, Ireland. So much action, so much dying, and Harvey Jackson always the indestructible one. And to go this way, at the final end of things.

The door slammed against the wall behind him. His hand was already groping for the butt of the Walther as he turned and found Stavrou and two armed men facing him.

"A tough bastard," Stavrou said. "I couldn't get a thing out of him."

"Yes, you train them well in the SAS, Major Villiers," Donner said. "I'll give you that."

Montera and Gabrielle were sitting by the fire talking together in low voices when the door opened and Donner entered. He closed it and came and stood with his back to the fire.

"This is nice. Damned cold out tonight."

"Have you been far?" Montera asked politely.

"Far enough. You see, I had a phone call early this evening from a friend in Paris. He'd been doing some checking for me on your girl friend here."

"What in the hell are you talking about?" Montera said angrily.

"Yes, Mademoiselle Legrand, or would you prefer Mrs. Gabrielle Villiers, or didn't you know she was married?"

"Divorced," Montera said. "Your information would appear to be hugely out of date."

Gabrielle sat there, frozen, waiting for the axe to fall. Donner said, "Yes, but who was Mr. Villiers, or should I say Major Villiers? Quite a man. Grenadier Guards and 22 SAS, would you believe? When my friend read his description to me over the phone a lot of interesting little pieces fell into place."

He crossed to the door, opened it, and Stavrou pushed his prisoner through. "Colonel Raul Montera, meet Major Anthony Villiers. I'd say you two have got a hell of a lot in common."

14

Two of Roux's men stood against the wall holding Armalite rifles. Stavrou gave Villiers another push farther into the room and tossed the Walther PPK across to Donner who caught it neatly.

"Found that strapped to his leg above the ankle."

Donner turned to Montera. "You see, a real pro. Of course, you do realize, Colonel, that this does raise a very big question as to sweet Gabrielle's role in this whole affair. I get the feeling she's not been strictly honest with you. I mean, the only possible explanation is that she's working quite hard for the other side."

Montera said to her calmly, "Is it true?"

"Yes," she said.

"Holy Mother!" he said. "I see it all now. It started in London, didn't it? Everything so convenient. And then Paris and the Bois."

Her eyes were hot, burning. She wanted to speak

and couldn't. She sat there staring at him. She opened her mouth, but no sound came.

It was Villiers who spoke for her. "Try and understand, Montera. She has a half brother, a helicopter pilot, killed flying off Stanley."

Her nails were digging into the palms of her hands with the strength of her emotion. She started to shake, and Raul Montera did a marvelous thing. He reached for the hands and held them tight, pulling her to her feet.

"It's all right," he said. "I understand. Be still." He spoke as if they were alone and put an arm around her shoulders.

Donner said, "My God, this really is cruelty to dumb animals." He crossed the room and flung open a green baize door. "In there, Colonel. Make your peace or do whatever you have to. I want words with the gallant major here anyway."

In Paris, Nikolai Belov was just about to retire for the night when the phone rang. Irana took the call.

"It's Donner for you," she said.

Belov took the phone from her. "How are things going?"

"More than interesting. Listen to this." Donner gave him a quick run-down on the evening's events. When he was finished, he said, "Have you done the usual search procedure on this one with your friends in French Intelligence?"

Although the scandal of the sapphire affairs had rooted out most KGB infiltration of the French Intelligence system, Belov still had agents in important positions there.

"We've run a most thorough check and it's right up to the minute. I only received the final report an hour ago. I'd intended phoning you in the morning. Not even a hint of your activities at any level in the system. No one waiting for you, no traps."

"But British Intelligence have certainly been on the ball. I wonder how."

"Surely the woman's involvement and her interest in Montera answers that. Montera was the link. She met him in London and then by chance, apparently, in Paris. But no accident at all, as we now see, and the time scale is such that it can only mean British Intelligence were expecting him to turn up. If we've been blown I would say it's occurred at the Argentina end and nowhere else."

"That makes sense."

"You still intend to proceed?"

"No reason not to."

"Fine, is there anything I can do for you?"

"Yes, as a matter of fact there is. I think it's time for a holiday back home in case there are any repercussions on this one. The Chieftain can make Finland with no problem. Can you recommend a suitable airfield to land at there?"

"Certainly. Perinö. We use it frequently. I'll see that arrangements are made for onward transportation. By the way, a news item of interest tonight. Professor Paul Bernard was discovered in a warehouse by the Seine, shot through the head."

"Is that a fact? Any juicy details?"

"The police are pursuing their inquiries. You know how it is?"

"I certainly do. I'll be in touch."

Belov put down the phone and sat there on the edge of the bed thinking. Irana said, "What is it?"

He smiled and held her hand. "I haven't taken any leave this year and neither have you. How would you like a trip to Moscow?"

"When?" she said.

"No time like the present. We could catch the Aeroflot flight at seven AM."

"I see. You have a bad feeling about this business?"

"Just a twinge, and I'm too old to take chances." He smiled again. "You better phone now and get the seats."

The room into which Donner had pushed Montera and Gabrielle was a kind of butler's pantry and wine store, and the window was heavily barred. She sat on a box and Montera lit a cigarette and waited.

She took a deep breath and looked up at him. "Can I tell you about it?"

"That might be a good idea."

"Tony and I were married for five years. We were divorced six months ago. Everything else I told you about myself is true. I missed out the fact that my mother is English and that she married again when I was quite small—an Englishman."

"Which explains the half brother."

"Yes. I've worked in journalism as I told you, but

I happen to have a gift for languages. I just soak them up. Always did, even as a child. Tony was frequently called upon to work with Group Four, that's the section of British Intelligence that deals with antiterrorism. The man who runs it approached me to work for them on a number of occasions. Nothing very heavy. Mainly my language ability."

"And I was one of these occasions?"

"Yes," she said flatly. "I was to try and find out if there was going to be any move against the Falklands."

He laughed out loud. "My God, I didn't know the first thing about it." He shook his head. "Serendipity again. The happiest of unlooked-for events."

"That's where it all went wrong," she said. "I didn't know what love was, and then I looked across the room at the Argentine Embassy and saw you."

"Yes, it was a rather splendid moment."

"And I couldn't get you out of my mind. Worried like hell about you when the war started, even though I'd no idea you were flying. And then this damned Exocet business started and the head man sent for me. You were the enemy, he said."

"And he was right."

"I was going to stop, just couldn't go on with the lies and the deceit after you gave me the ring."

"And then you heard about your brother?"

"I want it to stop, Raul," she said simply. "The killing on both sides, for all our sakes. If you take those Exocets back to Argentina tomorrow, it simply means more bloodshed."

He sighed heavily and shook his head. "My side is losing, Gabrielle. Maybe the Exocet is all we've got left. What do you want me to do? I'm an Argentinian. Your head man is right. I am the enemy."

She got up and moved to his side, and he slipped an arm around her waist.

"I'm tired, Raul, so tired. All I know for certain any more is that I love you."

Her head dropped on his shoulder. He kissed the golden hair and said nothing.

"What happens now?" Villiers asked when Donner came back into the sitting room. "More fun with cigarette lighters?"

"No need," Donner told him. "My sources in Paris have given me every assurance that I can proceed as planned. Were you responsible for seeing off poor old Paul Bernard, by the way?"

"Who's he?" Villiers asked.

"Yes, I thought so." Donner smiled. "What did he tell you? Convoys on the road to St. Martin? An ambush at dawn? Fairy stories for children, I assure you. I've something far better in mind." He poured himself a whisky. "And I wouldn't dream of damaging you at this stage of the game, Major. They'll want you intact at KGB headquarters in Moscow. What a mine of information you'll be, and don't tell me you won't talk. They have some remarkable drugs these days." He nodded to Stavrou. "Let's have the others back in here."

Stavrou opened the door of the butler's pantry, and

after a moment Montera and Gabrielle stepped out.

Montera said, "What do you intend to do with them?"

"More to the point is what I intend to do with you, Colonel."

There was silence. Montera waited, very calm. "Yes, I should have known there was more to this thing."

"Indeed there is. Major Villiers believed I would obtain Exocets for you by possibly ambushing an Aérospatiale convoy on the way to St. Martin tomorrow. The missiles are transshipped from there regularly to Île de Roc off the coast, which is a testing site."

"So?"

"And you are expecting a Hercules transport from Italy to touch down in the morning at Lancy with ten Exocets on board, courtesy of Colonel Qaddafi and the Libyans." He smiled. "Both wrong."

He crossed to a door in the far corner, opened it, and disappeared. He was back in a moment, putting on a French Army officer's tunic.

"Good fit, isn't it?" he said as he buttoned it up. "Allow me to introduce myself. Captain Henri Leclerc in charge of a detachment of nine men from the 23rd Guided Missile Regiment, proceeding by road, tomorrow morning, to St. Martin where a tank landing craft will be waiting to take us across to Île de Roc."

Villiers said, "Let me guess. They won't even get as far as St. Martin. You're going to work a switch?"

"Let's say we'll divert them to here and take over."

"And then proceed to Île de Roc?"

"There are only thirty-eight men on the island. I don't think we'll have much trouble. The gentlemen I've been keeping in the stables are very good at handling that sort of thing."

"And you simply take the Exocets you need from their testing stock?"

Donner nodded.

"You'll never get away with it," Villiers said.

"Why not? Once we take over, all we need is a couple of hours. On the right signal, a deep sea trawler comes in and takes off the missiles and the men. She sails under the Panamanian flag, by the way. Once out to sea she's just one more trawler, among the hundreds that fish those waters from every country in Europe."

Villiers, searching for a flaw, said, "There's bound to be a standard checking procedure between French Army Guided Weapon H.Q. and outstations. If they get radio silence from Île de Roc they'll want to know why."

"But they won't." Donner was enjoying himself. "We'll maintain essential radio contact. I've got an ex-army signals man on my staff for that very purpose. Another thing, emergency procedures don't come into operation until they've experienced radio silence for three hours. That gives us plenty of time."

And Raul Montera, who had listened to all this without speaking, his face hardening, said, "But this won't do and you know it."

"That's true. World opinion on such an action by the Argentinian Government will be one of horror. One can imagine the row in the United Nations, and God knows what the French will do."

"But this is not the action of the Argentinian Government," Montera said.

"Of course not, but as long as it appears to be, it's the same difference, and when the body of one of Argentina's greatest air aces is discovered after we're gone, that should clinch things nicely. Accidents will happen, stray bullets and so on." He poured himself another drink. "Why did you think I was so insistent on your government sending me someone like you in the first place?"

Montera was perfectly under control. "Why go to all this trouble?"

"Simple. You've lost the war already, my friend. If you had heard the news tonight, you would know that British paratroopers have won an astonishing victory at a place called Goose Green. The rest of their forces have started the long march to Port Stanley. I regret to have to say it, but they're the best trained soldiers in the world. Galtieri made a mistake. His government will fall anyway, but a scandal of the proportion I envisage will blow Argentina apart."

"Fear, chaos, and uncertainty," Villiers said. "The classic situation for your kind of takeover."

"Let's put it this way. The idea of units of the Russian fleet being able to operate in the South Atlantic from bases of a friendly power is certainly an intriguing one."

Gabrielle said, "You really are quite something, aren't you?"

"I told you I'd grow on you."

"And what happens afterward?" Villiers asked.

"Simple. The commanding officer at Île de Roc has a fast powerboat in which Stavrou and I will return to St. Martin. Once back, we fly out again in the Chieftain. First stop Finland, then the dear old homeland. That should be quite something. I haven't been back in years. As I told you, you'll go with me. They'll love you in Moscow. You, too, of course," he said to Gabrielle. "I couldn't very well leave you behind, now could I, and you're too good to break."

It was the first time that Montera's control snapped. He took a quick step forward, hands coming up. Stavrou grabbed an Armalite from one of the guards, reversed it quickly, and rammed the butt into the Argentinian's stomach. Montera went down.

Gabrielle rushed to his side, dropping to her knees. Donner laughed as he looked down at them.

"The only good thing I can say about the cellars here is that there's a lot of them, they're very secure, and the windows are barred. However, they are rather cold." He turned to Stavrou. "Put the three of them in together. An intriguing situation. They might have to bundle."

Wanda Jones had heard a great deal of what went on, sitting crouched beside the landing rail in the darkness above the main hall. She saw Stavrou and the two guards escort Villiers, Montera, and Gabrielle across to the door that she knew led to the cellars. After a while, Stavrou and one of the men returned. Donner appeared from the sitting room as the guard went out.

He said, "Everything okay?"

"Fine," Stavrou told him. "The doors on those cells are more than secure. Bolts an inch thick and I've left a guard in the corridor."

"Good," Donner said. "Warn the men for a six o'clock start and make sure Rabier stays sober."

"I will. What about Wanda?"

"Oh, yes, Wanda," Donner said. "I promised her something special. I've decided she can have you."

"You mean that?"

"Of course. I wish you well to wear it," Donner told him and returned to the sitting room.

Wanda felt physically sick as revulsion and fear coursed through her. As Stavrou hurried across the hall and started up the stairs, she got to her feet and moved along the landing in the darkness, blundering along the passageway beyond until she reached the door to the back stairs. As she opened it, light flooded out and Stavrou, at the end of the landing, saw her.

"Wanda!" he called.

She went through the door fast, slamming it behind her, and plunged down the stairs, kicking off her high-heeled shoes as she went. She managed to get the back door open, was outside and running across the lawn into the trees by the time he reached the bottom of the stairs.

She ran through the wood in total panic, head

down, an arm raised against flailing branches, and finally paused to listen. She could hear him blundering about some distance away on her right. He called her name angrily, and she moved away as quietly as possible. She had a sense, rather unclear, of which direction was inland, and she went that way steadily. Stavrou's voice faded out gradually, and soon the only sound she could hear, beneath the pelt and patter of raindrops, came from the twigs and branches that broke under her feet.

Stavrou said, "God knows where she's got to. Nothing but rain and darkness out there."

"Nowhere for her to go. She can't do us any harm," Donner said contemptuously, "I know my Wanda. The silly bitch will come crawling back when she's had enough of the rain. Better go and check the men out now."

Stavrou went and Donner tried the tunic on again. It really did fit him rather well. His official rank in the KGB was colonel. Once back in Moscow they'd probably promote him to general for services rendered. He wondered what *that* uniform would look like on him.

Gabrielle dozed in the corner of the cellar, Villiers's jacket about her shoulders. Montera took a cigarette from Villiers. As he gave Montera a light he said, "You remind me of an ad I used to see as a kid. It showed a man smoking a pipe and surrounded by beautiful women. It read, 'What's he got that other men haven't?" The answer was the brand of tobacco. What's your secret?"

"Relationships are really very simple," Montera said. "They either work or they don't. The moment you have to try hard, you've lost."

"Then I was in trouble from the beginning," Villiers admitted. "I seemed to spend all my time trying." He glanced across at Gabrielle. "A hell of a girl."

"I know," Montera told him.

"You would, wouldn't you," Villiers said bitterly, and went and sat in the corner, knees drawn up against his chest to conserve warmth.

They dozed fitfully and were finally awakened by the sound of footsteps in the courtyard. The first gray light of dawn seeped through the bars, and as Villiers looked out he saw a Land Rover drive out of the garage. Stavrou was at the wheel, Donner beside him. They were both in uniform. Montera joined Villiers and they watched the Land Rover turn out of the gate.

"It's started," Montera said.

"So it would appear."

Gabrielle stood up, pulling Villiers' jacket about her. "What are we going to do?"

"For the moment, nothing," Villiers told her. "Because there's nothing we can do."

The detachment from the 23rd Guided Missile Regiment traveled in a three-ton army truck, the officer sitting up front beside the driver. It was just after 6:00 A.M. and raining heavily when it came around a bend in the road near Lancy and found the Land Rover blocking the way. Donner, a military raincoat over his uniform, ran forward, waving his arms.

The truck slowed, the officer wound the window down and leaned out. "What is it?"

"Captain Leclerc?" Donner asked.

"That's right."

"Major Dubois, on assignment at Île de Roc at the moment. Crossed over to St. Martin last night with the landing craft to be ready to pick you up this morning, but this appalling rain is causing problems. Heavy flooding on the main road, so I thought I'd come to meet you with an alternative route."

"That's very good of you," Leclerc said.

"Not at all. Just follow the Land Rover and I'll have you there in no time."

Montera was standing at the window, peering out through the bars, when the Land Rover drove into the courtyard followed by the truck.

Villiers and Gabrielle moved to his shoulder. "Now what?" Villiers asked.

Donner and Stavrou got out of the Land Rover and Captain Leclerc jumped down to join them. He was a fair-haired young man with glasses, which were giving him trouble in the rain.

"Just exactly where are we?" he said.

The stable doors opened and Roux's men emerged on the run, every one in uniform and carrying either a rifle or a submachine gun. The whole thing was over in a few moments, the rest of the detachment ordered out of the back of the truck at gun point and hustled away with Leclerc.

Villiers turned to Montera. "Clever bastard, isn't he?"

They heard the sound of boots on the stone stairs outside, doors opening then closing again, bolts ramming home. Suddenly there was a movement at their own door. It was opened and Stavrou appeared, two men at his back.

"Right, Colonel, outside."

Montera hesitated. His hand reached for Gabrielle's, clung for a moment, then he moved out. She didn't say a word as the door slammed home and Villiers slipped an arm about her shoulders.

Outside, the footsteps receded along the corridor and mounted the steps. Villiers went to the tiny barred window in the door and on looking out found the young French officer he'd seen in the courtyard, peering through the bars of the opposite door.

"Who are you?" Villiers asked.

"Captain Henri Leclerc, 23rd Guided Missile Regiment. What in the hell is this all about?"

"I rather think they're substituting themselves for you and your men, so they land on Île de Roc."

"Good God," Leclerc said. "What for?"

So Villiers told him.

When he had finished, Leclerc said, "And how does he intend to leave here when he gets back?"

"He has a plane waiting at a bomber station up the road at Lancy. A Navajo Chieftain."

"He's certainly thought of everything."

"And not a damn thing we can do about it now. Even if we got out of here and put out a general alert, it would probably be too late. Aircraft can't land at Île de Roc. Even helicopters have problems."

"That's not quite true," Leclerc said. "I was very thoroughly briefed on the island before my posting, and there was considerable information on flying conditions, which interested me as I'm a pilot myself. Did a light aircraft course with the Army Air Corps. They experimented with landing small planes at the northern end of the island last year."

"But I thought there were cliffs there."

"True, but when the tide goes out it uncovers a large area of firm land. They found landing was no problem. Unfortunately the tide turns so quickly that it made the whole idea impracticable."

"It certainly is while we're stuck in here," Villiers said, and he kicked the door in frustration.

The last of Donner's men climbed into the rear of the truck. Donner, Stavrou, and Rabier, the pilot, stood at the bottom of the steps. Stavrou tied Montera's hands together in front of him with a black silk scarf.

"See how kind we're being," Donner said. "But the truth is, I don't want any telltale marks on your wrists when they find you."

"A true gentleman," Montera said, and then Stavrou stuffed a handkerchief into his mouth.

Donner said to Rabier. "Right, you're on your own. Those cellars are as impregnable as the Bastille, but keep an eye on them anyway. We should be back in five to six hours."

"Very well, Monsieur, you can rely on me."

"And if that bitch Wanda shows up, put her down in the cellar till I return."

Stavrou was by now at the wheel. "Ready when you are, sir."

Donner climbed into the truck, it moved away. Rabier turned and went up the steps into the house.

Wanda stood shivering behind a bush near the side of the road. Her hair was plastered wetly against her cheeks, her black velvet trouser suit was soiled and soggy. Across her shoulders, she held an old, brown horse blanket. She had spent the night in the woods, in a tiny ramshackle hut for hunters, and it had been far too cold for sleeping. She had been standing here for ten minutes trying to hitch a ride toward Paris.

Very faintly, the hum of an engine cut through the rain, and she tensed. Scrambling up to the side of the road, she raised an arm at a big, gray truck coming around a curve in the distance. Wanda would have stood in the middle of the road but was afraid of not being seen in the downpour. Suddenly, a thought went through her, and she froze. Could this be the truck the men were going to steal? She believed it. Her arm falling, she tumbled herself into the mud and leaf-filled ditch that ran beside the road. When she looked up, the truck was passing, and, through its glass, Donner's face flashed by.

The young woman climbed up out of the ditch

clutching her blanket and stood thinking and shivering. Then she walked down the road in the direction from which the truck had come. It only took her fifteen minutes to reach the Maison Blanc.

15

Donner stood in the wheelhouse of the land craft and looked through a porthole at the whole length of the ship. The hold was a steel shell. The cargo consisted of a large number of packing cases and the truck belonging to their own party, his men still inside. Beyond were the steel bow doors of the beaching exit.

The sea was choppy with a slight breeze, and although mist and rain had reduced visibility, they had made good time from St. Martin. The captain, a young naval lieutenant, came in from the bridge and gave the helmsman an order.

"Port five."

"Port five of wheel on, sir."

"Steady now."

"Steady, steering two-o-three, sir."

The lieutenant said to Donner, "Not long now. Another twenty minutes."

"Perhaps I'll have a chance to offer you a drink when we land?" Donner said.

The young man shook his head. "I'm only stopping long enough to put you and your party ashore, then I proceed to St. Nazaire. I'm carrying electronic equipment for Guided Weapons H.Q."

Donner nodded cheerfully. "Another time perhaps."

He went out on the bridge, wrapping the oilskin coat they had loaned him about his shoulders, and looked toward the great cliffs of Île de Roc rising out of the sea.

The harbor was not very large and the landing craft beached beside a stone jetty. One or two small sailing dinghies were pulled up on the sand above high water, but the only sizable craft was a beautiful powerboat, painted green.

When the bow doors opened, the truck drove out across a specially constructed concrete apron to the start of a macadam road, Donner walking beside it. A Land Rover was parked there and the sole occupant, a tall, graying middle-aged man wearing a jeep coat with a heavy fur collar over his uniform, got out.

"Captain Leclerc?"

"That's right," Donner said.

"Let's get out of this damned rain. Major Espinet—I'm in command here. I'll take you up to the site. Your truck can follow."

Donner nodded to Stavrou and got in. As the Land Rover moved away, he said to Espinet, "A beautiful boat down there in the harbor. Yours, I believe."

Espinet smiled. "The pride of my life. Built by

Akerboon. Steel hull, twin screws. She can do thirty-five knots."

"Wonderful," Donner commented.

"Helps pass the time in this Godforsaken spot," Espinet told him. "Not the most desirable of postings."

"That's what comes of losing the empire," Donner said amiably.

The winding road that led up from the harbor was lined with old stone cottages, most of which appeared to be in ruins. "Like most of these islands off the coast, the people left years ago," Espinet told him. "It was just subsistence living here. Farming and fishing. They seldom saw a ten-franc note from one year's end to the other."

They went over the hill above the harbor and there was the camp, a small, ugly compound of flat-roofed concrete huts built to withstand the fury of the storms that swept in from the Atlantic in the winter months. A concrete tower some forty feet in height lifted above them, a narrow balcony encircling its glass walls at the top, a steel emergency ladder running down one side.

Donner, who knew very well what it was, said, "What's that? The tower, I mean?"

"Built to house the radio room," Espinet said. "We also operate a new kind of short-wave scanner from up there when the missiles are testing. That's why we need height."

There was a row of bunkers some distance beyond. "Are those the missile pens?" Donner asked.

"That's right. They've got to be underground here. Nothing but Atlantic Ocean out there, which makes this an ideal test site, but the weather can be ferocious. Two winters ago it was so bad they evacuated for a month."

"They tell me half the people here are civilians?"

"That's right. Only eighteen military personnel at the moment. Three officers, so we don't have much of a mess, I'm afraid." Espinet turned the Land Rover into the complex. "You know, if you don't mind me saying so, there's something a little unusual about your accent."

"My mother," Donner said. "That's what's so unusual. She was Australian."

Espinet laughed. "That certainly explains it."

He braked to a halt outside one of the concrete huts, where two men in identical camouflage uniforms and black berets waited. One of them was a sergeant, the other wore captain's bars. As the captain came down to meet them Espinet said, "Pierre Jobert, my second-in-command."

They got out and Espinet made the introductions. Jobert, a pleasant, rather world-weary young man with a thin mustache, smiled as he shook hands. "Have you ever read *Beau Geste*, Captain Leclerc?"

"Naturally," Donner told him.

Jobert waved a hand that took in the entire complex. "Then you'll understand why we call this charming little hellhole Fort Zinderneuf. Coffee waiting in your office, sir."

238

"Excellent," Espinet said. "Assisted by a little cognac, I trust?" He turned to Donner. "Sergeant Deville will see to your men."

"I'll be right with you," Donner said. "Must have a word with them myself first."

The two officers went inside and Donner moved to where Stavrou waited beside the truck, which had parked some little distance away. "Montera still safely under wraps?"

"In back with the boys."

"Good. I'm going to have a drink with the C.O. The moment I'm inside, take care of the radio tower, then everything else stage by stage, just the way we discussed it. Only eighteen military personnel here at the moment. The rest are civilians. Less than I thought."

"Probably a few away on furlough," Stavrou said.

Donner smiled. "Lucky for them," and he turned and went up the steps to the door that Sergeant Deville held open for him.

Stavrou went around to the rear of the truck. The mercenary he had appointed as his second-in-command, a man named Jarrot, passed down a canvas bag. At that moment, Sergeant Deville joined them.

"Sergeants' mess first stop, then I'll drop off the rest of you."

Stavrou kneed him in the groin. As the sergeant started to go down, hands reached and hauled him into the back of the truck.

Stavrou said to Jarrot, "Okay, Claude, let's get moving."

Jarrot and Faure, the radio expert, jumped down, each carrying a canvas bag, and the three of them crossed to the base of the radio tower; Stavrou opened the door and led the way up the narrow spiral staircase to the top. When he stepped out on to the narrow balcony, the wind tried to push him against the wall and he grabbed for the rail with his free hand. He could see the harbor clearly, but beyond, the sea was shrouded with mist, as was the higher part of the island.

Jarrot and the other man pushed up behind him and they looked in through the armored glass of the door to the communications room. There were three operators in there, two technical sergeants sitting at a desk in the center.

They looked up in surprise as the three men opened the door and filed in. Stavrou dumped his bag on the desk between the sergeants, scattering their papers.

He grinned impudently. "Good day to you, boys," he said. He unzipped the bag and took out a Schmeisser machine pistol. "This is what got the SS through the Second World War. Still does its job very well, so don't waste my time in arguing."

One of the sergeants jumped up, reaching for the holstered pistol at his belt, and Jarrot, who had produced an AK assault rifle from his holdall, smashed the butt against the side of the man's head. He went down with a groan.

The remaining sergeant and the three radio operators got their hands up fast. Stavrou reached in his holdall and produced a number of steel handcuffs which he tossed on the table.

"Surplus stock, French military prisons for the use of." He was thoroughly enjoying himself. "We got them cheap." He turned to Jarrot. "Right, Claude, you can do the honors."

Within a couple of minutes, the four soldiers lay on the floor, face down beside the unconscious one, all with their wrists handcuffed behind their backs. Faure was already examining the radio equipment.

"Any problems?" Stavrou asked.

Faure shook his head. "Most of it is standard military stuff."

"Good. You know what to do. Get in touch with the trawler, tell them it's safe to move in and get me an estimated time of arrival."

"Okay." Faure sat down at one of the sets.

Stavrou turned to Jarrot. "Eighteen military personnel in all, that's what Mr. Donner said. Five down—eleven to go." He grinned. "Let's visit the sergeants' mess next, Claude. You lead the way."

Donner, standing at the window of Major Espinet's office, a glass of cognac in hand, watched the two men emerge from the door at the base of the radio tower. They moved to the truck, Stavrou climbed up behind the wheel, Claude stood on the running board, and they moved away.

Donner said, "When do you intend to put us to work, Major?"

"No rush," Espinet said. "Got to get acclimatized. All the time in the world in a bloody place like this."

"Not for me there isn't—time, I mean." Donner produced a Walther from his pocket, a heavy silencer screwed on the end.

Espinet stood up behind his desk, eyes bulging. "What in the hell is going on?"

"Quite simple," Donner said. "I'm taking over."

"You must be mad." Espinet turned to Jobert. "Pierre, phone the guardroom."

Donner shot the major through the back of the head, knocking him back across his chair into the corner, killing him instantly. The obscenity of his death was intensified by the almost complete lack of sound from the silenced Walther.

Jobert said, "Who are you, for God's sake?"

Donner said, "You can use your intelligence. Sufficient to say that my country is at war and we need more Exocets. I've got a boat coming in here soon and we're going to take as many as we can lay our hands on and you're going to help."

"Like hell, I will," Jobert said.

"Oh, all very gallant and French are we today?" Donner touched the end of the silencer between his eyes. "You'll do exactly as you're told because if you don't, I'll parade your entire unit and shoot every third man."

And Jobert believed him, which was the important thing, sudden despair in his eyes, shoulders sagging.

242

Donner poured himself another brandy and toasted him.

"Cheer up, sport," he said. "After all, you could be like Espinet. You could be dead. Now let's get moving."

They went up the street together to where the truck was parked outside one of the huts. Stavrou and Jarrot were emerging from another hut on the left and they all met together as three more of the mercenaries came out of the hut opposite.

Stavrou said, "Five in the radio room, six in the sergeant's mess, two corporals in the office of that hut opposite. Every man on his face in steel bracelets."

"Which leaves three military personnel unaccounted for." Donner turned to Jobert. "Where are they, Captain?"

Jobert hesitated, but only for a moment. "On duty in the missile pen."

"Good. Now for the civilians. Twenty of them, isn't that right?"

"I suppose so."

"How many of them in the pens at the moment?"

"Probably five. They work shifts. The others will be eating or sleeping."

"Excellent. Then if you'll be good enough to lead the way, we'll introduce ourselves, shall we?"

Rabier was sitting at the kitchen table eating bread and cheese and drinking cognac. He had been drinking for a long time, and for half that time Wanda had been watching him from the loft in the stable where she was huddling in the straw and drying herself off.

Wanda was still cold and hungry, but she felt more determined now. She knew the only one guarding the Maison Blanc was Rabier. Moving to the corner of the loft, she opened a trapdoor and descended a flight of wooden steps. Now she was in the stables Roux's men had used as their quarters. There were sleeping bags in the stalls and various items of equipment laid out on a trestle table, including an assortment of weapons.

She opened the door and looked outside. It was still raining and she tiptoed cautiously across the cobbles toward the kitchen door. Gabrielle, who had been peering out through the cellar window, saw her coming.

"Wanda!" she whispered urgently. "Over here."

Villiers was on his feet in a second. "What is it?"

Wanda crossed to the wall and crouched down at the window. "They've all gone except Rabier, the pilot."

"I know," Gabrielle said. "Come down and let us out as fast as you can."

Wanda nodded, stood up, and hurried to the back door. She opened it cautiously and started along the passage, pausing at the kitchen door, which stood ajar. Rabier stood at the kitchen table opening a fresh bottle of cognac. Wanda tiptoed past and opened the door into the hall. It creaked slightly in spite of the care with which she closed it, and in the kitchen,

Rabier paused in the act of pouring cognac into a glass and listened, a slight frown on his face, head cocked to one side. He went out into the passage, still holding the bottle of cognac.

Wanda paused in the hall for a moment. The house was silent and she crossed to the door leading to the cellar steps, opened it, and went down. She felt for the light switch at the bottom and whispered, "Gabrielle, where are you?"

"Here, Wanda! Here!" Gabrielle called.

Wanda hesitated at the cellar door, peering in through the bars, aware of Gabrielle inside, Villiers at her shoulder. There was a great rusting bolt at the top of the door which pulled back without too much difficulty, but the other bolt at the bottom of the door was a different proposition. She got on her knees, tugging at it with both hands, and suddenly there was a movement behind her, a hand fastened in her hair, pulling her head back painfully, dragging her to her feet. She twisted around to find Rabier smiling at her.

"Naughty," he said. "Very naughty. I can see I'm going to have to take you in hand."

He was very drunk and thrust the neck of the cognac bottle into her mouth painfully so that she choked as the fiery liquid poured down her throat. He laughed again, unpleasantly, eyes fixed, an ugly look on his face, and put the bottle on a shelf beside them.

"And now," he said, "I'll teach you how to do as you're told," and forced his mouth on hers, holding her against the wall, one hand still fastened in her hair, the other pawing at her breasts.

Gabrielle cried out in anger and then Villiers pulled her to one side, reached through the bars with one hand and got Rabier by the hair, yanking him back against the door with considerable force.

"The bottle, Wanda!" he ordered. "The bottle."

For Wanda, Rabier was every man who had ever used her, the humiliation of the years welling up in a killing rage. She grabbed for the neck of the cognac bottle and clubbed Rabier across the side of the head. He cried out, staggering, and she hit him again, sending him to his knees. She kicked him out of the way, the rage in her so strong that this time when she reached for the bolt, it opened with no difficulty, and Gabrielle and Villiers moved out to join her.

When the phone rang, Ferguson was just out of the shower. He listened to Villiers, then said, "Right, Tony. You stay where you are. Let the French handle it now. Good work."

He slammed down the phone and ran into the sitting room, clutching the towel around him.

"Harry, where the devil are you?"

Fox appeared from the study. "You wanted me, sir?"

"Tony's cracked it. Now all we need is some fast action from the French. Get Colonel Guyon in Paris for me now. Top priority. Most urgent."

He ran back into his bedroom and started to dress.

* * *

Rabier was tied up and bundled into the butler's pantry and Villiers helped himself to the Walther he carried. "I should imagine the brigadier's on to Paris now."

"It will still take time for them to move," Gabrielle said. "What about Raul? You've got to do something, Tony."

"Yes, I know." Villiers turned to Leclerc. "Are you game to fly the Chieftain out to Île de Roc and try landing her on that beach."

Leclerc smiled. "It would certainly give Donner one hell of a surprise, and we could take half a dozen of my men."

Villiers turned to look at them. They seemed fit enough, but rather more intellectual than the average soldier, and two of them wore glasses.

"These boys are technicians, aren't they? Electronics wizards?"

"And good soldiers, too, believe me. What we lack are weapons."

Wanda said, "There are rifles and things in the stables where those men of Donner's were staying. I just saw them."

Leclerc turned to his men. "Come on then. What are we waiting for?" And he led the way out.

Gabrielle put a hand on Villiers's arm. "Take care, Tony, and try to be in time."

"I will." On impulse he kissed her on the forehead. He walked to the door.

She called, "Tony?"

He turned, "Yes?"

"I think you were always worth something better."

"Than you?"

"Oh, no. I'm still too arrogant to admit that." She smiled. "Than what you do, Tony. You're worth so much more than Ferguson and all his dark games. Worth a little joy. And I'm sorry about us—sorry about a lot of things."

He smiled, looking suddenly as charming as on the first time she'd met him. "I'm not. When the going was good, it was bloody marvelous. I wouldn't have missed you for anything."

He went out. A moment later she heard the Peugeot start up and move away, and then there was only the silence.

In Espinet's office, Raul Montera sat in a chair, hands still bound by the silk scarf. The major lay in the corner covered by a blanket. Donner turned from a cupboard and held up a bottle of champagne.

"The old devil did himself well. Krug '71. An exceptional year. Pity there isn't time to chill it. Still, you can't have everything in this life." He thumbed off the cork and laughed as the champagne foamed. "You'll join me in a glass?"

"As you well know, it doesn't agree with me," Montera said calmly.

"Well, it agrees with me, old sport." Donner filled a glass and went to the window and peered out. "Things have certainly gone well, you must admit. Nothing like a little organization."

"I heard some shooting."

"Just a little. A couple of guards up at the missile pens loosed off a few rounds before my boys cut them down. Very useful that. It makes it all hang together when we leave you face down with a bullet in you, from one of their weapons, naturally."

The door opened and Stavrou entered.

Donner said, "Have you made contact with the trawler?"

"Yes, they should be here in thirty-five minutes."

"Everything else under control?"

"Everyone under lock and key except for ten civilian personnel who are loading Exocets onto trucks in the missile pens, under supervision."

"Excellent," Donner said. "You get back up there and keep things moving. We'll join you in a few minutes. The colonel might find it interesting."

Stavrou went out. Donner refilled his glass and raised it in mock salute to Montera as rain rattled the window.

"Not long now, old sport."

Sitting in the cockpit of the Chieftain beside Leclerc, Villier saw Île de Roc lift out of the sea on the horizon, a gray hump under cumulus clouds, the cliffs at the northern end wreathed in mist. They were flying at no more than three hundred feet above the sea. Leclerc's hands steady on the column, and below, the gray-green surface was being whipped into whitecaps.

Villiers said, "What about wind direction? Will it be all right for landing?"

"Good enough, I think. It's the downdrafts from those cliffs we'll have to watch for."

The island crouched there like a gray beast, waiting for them, the great cliffs rearing three hundred feet high at one end, the rest of the desolate land mass sloping steeply toward the harbor.

"You realize they'll know we're coming?" Leclerc said. "No way of avoiding that."

"I know," Villiers said. "It can't be helped so you might as well cut right in across the island and let's see the state of the game. A little panic and confusion always helps."

The Chieftain went in across the cliffs, the mist parting before it, roaring across a desolate, rain-soaked moonscape, a nightmare world of deep gullies fissured into gray rock, the occasional green of bog or moorland. Leclerc pulled back on the column and they lifted over a ridge and found the missile pens, the concrete buildings of the camp complex no more than a hundred feet below.

Donner and Raul Montera were walking up the street toward the missile pens. Donner glanced up in alarm, then pushed Montera into a stumbling run toward the shelter of the tunnel entrance leading to the pens. Leclerc banked, came in again at fifty feet this time, then turned and moved out to sea.

Stavrou had observed the whole incident from the shelter of the tunnel entrance, and as Donner and Montera ran in beside him, he said, "I don't understand. That was our plane. What in the hell is going on?"

"Villiers, you imbecile," Donner said. "Who else could it be. God knows what's gone wrong back there at the house."

He looked out from the tunnel entrance to where the Chieftain banked over the sea and came in again, heading for the cliffs and disappearing from view.

"What the hell are they doing?" Stavrou said. "Nowhere to land on this rock."

"Oh yes there is," Donner said. "If the tide's right, there's plenty of beach at the base of those cliffs. The French Air Force proved it could be done last year. It just wasn't a practical proposition on a long-term basis, that's all."

"So what do we do?" Stavrou said. "If that is Villiers, then he must have contacted the French authorities. We could have paratroopers around our necks before we know it."

"Let's see how things are inside," Donner said.

He pushed Montera ahead of him and they moved along the tunnel and entered a large concrete cave brightly lit by floodlights. Four of the special trucks built to carry the missiles were lined up at a loading ramp where the civilian personnel in Aérospatiale overalls toiled to load the Exocets with the assistance of special hydraulic hoists, closely supervised by armed mercenaries.

Jarrot was in charge, and Donner said, "What stage are you at?"

"Difficult to say. With luck, another twenty minutes and we can move down to the harbor."

Donner turned to Stavrou. "I'll stay here. You take

some men and get up on those cliffs. If anyone is trying to get through, stop them. You must give us the time we need."

Stavrou grinned savagely. "My personal guarantee on it." He nodded to Jarrot. "Come on, Claude. We've got work to do."

They ran back along the tunnel. Donner took out a cigarette and lit it. "Villiers," he said. "How incredible." He laughed, totally without malice. "God damn him, he must be nearly as good as me."

"What was it you said?" Montera asked. "Nothing like a little organization."

"One of those days," Donner said amiably. "Everyone has them."

"So now what happens?"

"We wait and see, old sport, but preferably back in Espinet's office in comfort. I left that bottle of Krug on his desk and it's too good to waste, chilled or not."

Leclerc took the Chieftain in on a trial run, feeling for the wind. A crosscurrent from the island caught them so that they rocked violently in the turbulence. He brought the Chieftain around in a tight circle and came in low over the waves, throttling back and dropping flaps.

The wheels seemed to touch the surface of the water and then they were down, biting into the hard, wet sand and running forward through the shallows, spray flying up in great clouds on either side. Leclerc taxied to the far end of the beach, turned into the wind, and switched off the engines.

"The tide's on the turn. Maybe an hour and there won't be enough beach left for a takeoff."

"It doesn't matter," Villiers told him. "After all, it isn't our plane."

He produced the Walther he had taken from Rabier, checked the action, then put it back in his pocket. Leclerc's men had already got the air-stair door open and were scrambling out onto the beach one by one, each man taking with him a weapon from the supply of arms they had brought from Maison Blanc. Villiers picked up an Armalite, slipped a hand grenade into his pocket, and joined them.

A cold wind drove rain in across the wet sand flats as they stood around him in a semicircle. "How many of you have had combat experience?" he demanded.

Leclerc indicated a tall, fit looking young man with close-cropped hair whose steel-rimmed glasses were already misting with rain. "Sergeant Albray here was on detachment with the Foreign Legion in Chad two years ago. He's been under fire more than once. As for the rest of us . . ." He shrugged.

"All right," Villiers said. "There's only time for me to say one thing of importance to you in the circumstances. No Boy Scout ethics like giving those bastards a fair chance. Shoot them in the back if you have to because that's exactly what they'll do to you. Now let's get out of here," and he turned and started to run across the sand toward the base of the cliffs.

They had seemed impregnable on the flight in from the sea, but on a closer view, an enormous gully could be seen, water running down the center. It provided an easy if strenuous route up from the beach.

Ten minutes later they were over the top and starting down the slope through a jumble of broken gray boulders, sparse grass, everything shrouded in clinging mist. Villiers sensed voices somewhere below, held up his hand to caution Leclerc and the others to silence.

They went forward through the mist and came to the edge of an escarpment. There below, toiling up the slope, was Jarrot, followed by three other men. Villiers had eyes only for Stavrou bringing up the rear, could see only Harvey Jackson's tortured face as he sat tied to the chair in that wretched little bungalow near Lancy.

He took the grenade from his pocket and pulled the pin with his teeth. For once, anger betrayed his usual icy calm and rigorous training.

"Stavrou, you bastard!" he called. "Here's a present from Harvey Jackson," and he tossed the grenade into the ravine.

Stavrou, alerted by that cry, every instinct bred of years of hard living coming to his aid, was already turning, diving headlong down the hillside, rolling out of sight into the mist and rain. Not so his companions. There was a shattering explosion followed by screams, and Villiers moved to the edge, his Armalite ready. The ravine was like a butchershop, Jarrot and his three companions all badly hit, and there was horror on the faces of the young French soldiers as they moved to join Villiers. He raised the Armalite to his shoulder and fired at one of the men who was trying to crawl away.

Leclerc caught him by the shoulder and swung him around. "For God's sake, haven't you had enough?"

There was a single shot, a bullet caught Leclerc in the side of the head, splintering bone as it emerged above his right ear, and he fell back over the edge.

One of the sergeants, bracing himself on one knee, loosed off a long burst from his machine pistol at Jarrot, who had fired the shot from the hip. The bullets spun him around and shredded the back of his camouflage jacket so that it burst into flame.

There was only silence then as they stood beside Villiers, staring at the carnage and at Leclerc's body down there also.

"Is that it, sir?" one of the young sergeants asked.

Villiers shook his head. "There are still others down there at the base and the man we really want, Felix Donner. I'm sorry about your captain. He was a good man, but you don't survive in war by being either kind, decent, or honorable, not these days. I hope you've learned your lesson. Use it well when we get down there." He slammed another clip into his Armalite. "All right, follow me, do exactly as I say and you might just live forever."

Donner, back in Espinet's office, heard the grenade explosion and then the rattle of small-arms fire that followed it. He moved to the window, glass in hand, and saw Stavrou running down the slope on the other side of the huts.

Montera said, "Could something else have gone wrong, do you think?"

Donner turned around, still smiling, but the eyes were cold and very dark. He said, "You really do presume on my good nature, old sport, don't you?" He took a quick step forward and punched Montera in the face, catching him high on the right cheek, sending him flying backward out of the chair.

He opened the door and stepped outside as Stavrou ran across the street toward the entrance to the tunnel to the missile pens. Stavrou saw him at once and veered toward him.

"How bad?" Donner demanded.

"Villiers caught us in a ravine up there. Had at least half a dozen men with him."

"Jarrot and the others?"

"Grenade. I only got out myself by the skin of my teeth. What do we do now?"

Donner appeared to consider the matter, although he had already made his decision, at least as regards his own future. A shambles, no other word for it, and one thing was certain. The presence of Villiers and his men meant that much stronger forces wouldn't be far behind. Last stands were for fools, and the

Chieftain on the beach at the foot of those cliffs was a much more attractive proposition.

He said to Stavrou, "Get up to the radio room, Yanni, and contact the captain of the trawler. Don't, whatever you do, tell him what the situation is or the bastard will simply turn tail and get the hell out of it. Just tell him my orders are to come ahead at his best possible speed. Once that's sorted out, get the others. I'll meet you down at the harbor."

"And the Exocets?" Stavrou demanded.

"Yesterday's news. If we get out of this one in one piece we've done well. Off you go!"

Stavrou went out. Montera said, "You can say I'm a cynic, but I get the impression you've just sold our friend right down the river."

"He shouldn't have joined." Donner reached for the bottle of Krug. "Might as well finish this."

"There's nowhere to go," Montera said softly. "It's over, or hasn't that sunk in yet?"

"There's always somewhere to go, sport, especially when you have a plane on the beach and the pride of the Argentine Air Force to fly it for you."

He emptied his glass in one quick swallow and hurled it into the corner to smash against the wall.

Villiers ordered his men to stay down and moved to the edge of the escarpment in time to see Stavrou cross to the radio tower, open the door, and disappear inside. The entire base was laid before them like a map.

Villiers pointed to the tunnel entrance to the missile pens. "Presumably you were briefed before this posting," he said to Sergeant Albray. "Would that be where the Exocets are?"

"That's right," Albray said. "The radio room is at the top of the tower."

There was another long, low concrete building to the right, where two of Donner's men appeared to be standing guard.

"And that?" Villiers demanded.

"As I remember from the plans, that's the fuel store."

Villiers nodded. "They've probably got most of the personnel on the base imprisoned in there."

"No sign of the trawler," Albray said, looking down toward the harbor.

"Probably on her way in right now. Even if Donner thinks things have gone badly wrong, he won't want to be left stranded. On the other hand, he might decide to go all Russian on us and sacrifice himself for the sake of the dear old motherland. Order that trawler to get the hell out of it, which would be a pity. Nice to think it's going to end up in the bag with everybody else."

"So what do we do?" Albray asked.

"We'll tackle the tower, you and I. Probably only the creep who just went in, Stavrou, and a radio operator up there." He turned to the rest of the soldiers. "Give Sergeant Albray and me five minutes, then move in and move in hard. Take out those two guards at the fuel store, then block the mouth of that tunnel. Anyone tries to move out, shoot the hell out of them and remember what I said. Don't give the bastards a chance because they won't give you one."

They skirted the back of one of the concrete huts and paused in its shelter, no more than ten yards from the tower. Villiers pointed to the steel ladder running up the outside of the tower to the balcony.

He moved forward and, holding the Walther ready in his right hand, started to climb. Albray waited until he was ten or fifteen feet high and ran forward, opened the door at the base of the tower and went inside.

As he did so, Yanni Stavrou came around the final bend of the spiral staircase. The gun on his hip was holstered, but his reflexes were excellent. He took in Albray, the uniform, in a split second, was already turning and running back out of sight as the sergeant fired his machine pistol. Albray, without the slightest hesitation, went after him.

Villiers was more than halfway up the ladder when he heard the shooting from inside the tower. He paused, hanging on with one hand, the Walther in his other hand. He looked down, and again everything moved in on him as that dreadful fear of heights returned.

The guards outside the fuel store, looking up, started to raise their weapons, and then Leclerc's men emerged from between two concrete huts opposite, firing as they came, cutting them down from behind.

Above Villiers, the radio operator leaned over the rail, a machine pistol in his hand, and Villiers fired one-handed, the reflexes of hard training taking over, all fear leaving him. The man cried out and staggered back out of sight as Villiers started to climb again.

Donner ran to the window, drawing his revolver, and looked out as firing erupted in the street.

Raul Montera laughed softly. "I think that perhaps this time you've left things a little late, my friend."

Donner didn't bother to reply, simply opened the door a crack and peered out. The two guards at the fuel store lay in the street outside and one of Leclerc's men was unlocking the door. There was gunfire at the other end of the street and he saw two of his men fleeing toward the harbor.

He closed the door calmly, and pulling Montera to his feet pushed him into the kitchen at the rear. Then, opening the back door, he said, "Now get moving!" and shoved the Argentinian outside.

Villiers peered over the edge of the balcony, cautiously, but there was no one there except for the dead radio operator sprawled against the wall, the machine pistol on the floor beside him. Villiers picked up the machine pistol and moved to the radio room's door, which swung in the wind, but there was no one there.

There was a quick step behind him, he swung, the machine pistol coming up as Stavrou paused in the doorway, an automatic in one hand. The look on his face said everything, rage for a brief moment, then the cold calculation of the professional survivor. He assessed his chances against the machine pistol and made his decision. He laid down his automatic very carefully, Villiers raised the machine pistol, finger tightening on the trigger and Stavrou smiled. "Oh no you won't, Major Villiers. I mean, it wouldn't be British, would it? Playing fields of Eton and all that fair play stuff."

Villiers moved in close. "You mean I'm a gentleman?"

"Something like that."

The bone-handled fisherman's gutting knife that Stavrou had carried in his right sleeve for years slipped into the palm of his hand, there was a click as his thumb found the button, the arm swept up, the blade streaking for the soft flesh beneath Villiers' chin.

And Villiers, anticipating just such a move, praying for it, dropped his machine pistol, blocked the arm with practiced skill, grabbed for the wrist with both hands, twisting it cruelly so that Stavrou dropped the knife and cried out in pain. Villiers wrenched the arm around and up, still keeping that terrible hold in position, and this time Stavrou screamed as muscles tore, was still screaming as Villiers ran him headfirst through the door and out across the rail to plunge forty feet to the concrete below.

It was at that precise moment that Donner and Montera emerged from the back of the officers' mess. Stavrou's body hit the ground at the base of the tower and Donner looked up to see Villiers appear at the rail, Sergeant Albray behind him. The sergeant raised his machine pistol to fire and Donner pulled Montera in front of him as a shield.

On the balcony Villiers held the sergeant's arm. "No, leave it to me." He turned and went down the spiral staircase on the run.

Donner and Montera went up the ravine at the rear of the camp and emerged on the upper slope. They started across the plateau toward the edge of the cliff, Donner pushing the Argentinian in front of him.

"I told you, there's no place to run," Montera said.

"Oh yes there is. You're going to fly us out of here, Colonel."

They reached the edge of the cliffs and the Chieftain was clearly visible in spite of the mist, strangely alien in such a place. There was only one thing wrong. The sea rolled in across the sand in great, hungry breakers. Already at least half the area on which the Chieftain had landed was eaten away, the rest broken up by great trailing fingers of salt water.

"You've had it," Montera said. "See for yourself."

"Get moving!"

Donner pushed him down into the gully and they went sliding down together in a shower of broken stones and earth. They plunged down the final slope of scree and emerged onto the open beach, aware at once of the strong fresh wind blowing in from the sea.

Montera had ended up on his back, hampered by

his bound hands. As Donner pulled him to his feet a cascade of stones rained down from above. Donner turned, firing into the mist blindly, then grabbed Montera by the collar and ran for the plane, pushing him in front of him.

As they reached the Chieftain, he rammed Montera against the side and pushed the revolver barrel up under his chin. Then he took a knife from his pocket, sprang the blade, and sliced through the silk scarf.

He stood back. "Okay, inside and let's get out of here."

Montera's face stayed calm, but it was something in the eyes that made Donner turn to find Tony Villiers arriving on the run, traveling fast, the Walther in his right hand. He halted perhaps thirty feet away.

"All right, Donner, let him go!" he called.

Donner, half-turned toward Montera, sighed. "Like I said, it's been one of those days."

Montera said, "Don't try it, not with him."

"Maybe you've got a point," Donner said. "On the other hand. I'm tired of running, sport."

He turned, the revolver swinging up in his right hand. Villiers fired three times very fast, one bullet catching Donner in the right shoulder, spinning him around, the others shattering his spine, driving him against the plane. He bounced off and fell on his face and a wave swept in over him from the incoming tide, lapping around the wheels of the plane.

Montera stood looking at him. "Nothing like a little organization," he said softly.

"What's that?" Villiers asked.

"Nothing important. Is Gabrielle all right?"

"Yes, fine, waiting back at Maison Blanc. We had a certain amount of luck there. Wanda Jones released us, the rest we made up as we went along."

"Who flew the plane?"

"The French captain, Leclerc."

There was a distant buzzing, and Montera pointed to where three helicopters moved in under low cloud, line astern.

"Who's that?"

"The French, unless I'm very much mistaken, arriving just too late. Probably paratroopers. Do you think you could fly this thing out of here?"

Montera looked about him. "We haven't got a clear run. It's all broken up by water channels, as you can see. Why do you ask?"

"Because I think it might be a good idea if you got the hell out of here, and in the circumstances, I'm willing to take my chances with you. There's going to be one hell of a row about this and I'd rather be out of it. And I don't owe the French anything. They sold you the Exocets that sank the *Sheffield*, *Coventry*, and *Atlantic Conveyor* in the first place."

"They also sold them to you, my friend."

"True. Which goes to prove something. Come on, are we going or are we not? You can only die once."

"Okay," Montera said. "You're on."

He climbed in behind the controls, and Villiers got into the passenger seat beside him and secured the door. The engines coughed into life with a shattering roar, drowning every other sound.

"What do you think?" Villiers shouted.

Montera didn't even bother to reply. There was a strange, set smile on his face. He taxied into the wind and gave the plane full throttle. The Chieftain shuddered and seemed to leap forward on a diagonal course to the sea, which gave them the longest strip of beach left.

They went across one water channel and then another and another, spray flying up in clouds on either side, Montera stamping hard on the rudder bar to keep her straight. And then she lifted, one wing dipping slightly, and the breakers were beneath them, the wheels skimming the whitecaps.

Quite suddenly, they were moving very fast indeed, the engine note deepening into a full-throated roar, and only then did Montera pull back on the control column.

After a couple of hours of waiting at the house, Gabrielle could take it no longer, and she and Wanda walked to the airfield. It was still raining hard and they sheltered in the hangar.

Gabrielle said, "What are you going to do after this?"

Wanda shrugged. "God knows. I was on the street when Felix picked me up. It was like a dream. From the gutter to luxury, just like that. I suppose I'll just have to wake up now." She shook her head. "He was a right bastard, you know that? And I was so afraid of him."

"Then why did you stay?"

"Because I was more afraid of being back on the street."

"And now?"

Wanda said, "Oh, I don't know. All of a sudden, it looks as if it could be interesting."

"I've been thinking," Gabrielle said. "I've got a lot of good friends in the magazine business, and I've got a hunch the camera would like you. Maybe we could put something together."

"You mean, Wanda Jones as a sort of *Vogue* centerfold?" Wanda grinned. "Now that really would be something."

There was the sound of engines in the far distance and the Chieftain came in low from the west, then turned into the wind for landing.

Wanda said, "I've just thought of something. What if it isn't them? What if they lost out? It could be Felix."

Gabrielle turned, astonishment on her face. "You really think a man like Donner could take Tony Villiers?" She laughed out loud. "My God, Wanda, but you do have a lot to learn," and she turned and walked toward the plane as it taxied in.

The Chieftain came to a halt, but Montera didn't switch off the engine, simply sat there staring out of the windscreen.

He said, "Could you make it fast? I want to get out of here."

"You're not staying?"

"Nothing to stay for."

"I'd say there is, standing right outside by the port wing."

Montera slid back the side window and looked out at her. Gabrielle was laughing, all the relief in the world in her face. She waved excitedly.

He turned to Villiers. "Please, Tony."

It was the first time he had used his name and there was anguish in his voice. Villiers said, "Okay, but I'm sticking with you. Where are we going?"

"Where we started from. Brie Comte Robert."

"And then?"

"There's an Air France jumbo leaving for Buenos Aires tonight. I intend to be on it."

He started to turn the Chieftain away, increased speed. Gabrielle wasn't smiling now, her mouth opening in a cry that was soundless, drowned by the roaring of the engines. Then she was somewhere behind, and the end of the runway was rushing toward them.

The concourse at Charles de Gaulle Airport was not particularly busy as Tony Villiers waited by the bookstand outside the international departure lounge. Montera was at the Air France desk checking his bag through. He turned and paused to light a cigarette, a curiously elegant figure in the old black flying jacket and the jeans.

"Dear God," Villiers said softly, "I actually like the man. Everything all right?" he asked as Montera approached.

"I've got to change at Rio. Something to do with flying in the exclusion zone. Obviously no one intends to take any chances. No problem. Even allowing for that, I should be in Buenos Aires within seventeen or eighteen hours."

"And then what? Back to Rio Gallegos and that Skyhawk Squadron?"

"What do you think?"

"That you're exactly that kind of holy fool. You've lost the war, Raul. It's over. You saw the evening papers. We're on our way. Those Commandos are walking across East Falkland to Stanley. Everybody said it couldn't be done, but they're doing it. The only thing standing between the British Army and total victory is maybe nine or ten thousand men dug in around Stanley and what's left of your air force."

"Exactly. While I've been playing games up here in Europe, the rest of my boys have been getting blown out of the sky down there in the South Atlantic."

"So you want to join them?" Villiers was surprised to find he was actually angry. "I know, don't tell me. A matter of honor."

"Something like that."

"And Gabrielle? She loves you, you know that, and where she's concerned, I'm an expert. Oh, a failed expert, perhaps, but I know this. She never looked at me like she looks at you. I never saw her smile like that."

"There's nothing left for Gabrielle and me, not after what's happened," Montera said.

"Can't you understand?" Villiers told him. "She was in a hole she couldn't get out of. Ferguson held all the cards."

Montera laughed. "I understand perfectly, but there's her brother to be considered." He shivered slightly. "He would always be between us, Tony, can't you see that?"

His name was called over the loudspeaker. He dropped his cigarette, put his foot on it and smiled. "That's it, then."

He held out his hand and Villiers took it for a moment. "Good luck. I'm afraid you're going to need it."

"What the hell does it matter as long as it's quick?" Montera moved to the gate and turned. "Do your best for her, Tony," and then he was gone.

Villiers went into the bar, sat in the corner, and ordered coffee and a cognac. He felt restless and out of sorts. Damn the man. As he'd kept saying himself, he *was* the enemy, and yet it seemed such a waste. He had another cognac, then went out, found an international call box, and phoned the Cavendish Square number.

Ferguson said, "You're phoning from Charles de Gaulle, I presume? You've seen Raul Montera off?"

"How in the hell did you know?" Villiers demanded.

"Pierre Guyon and Section Five of the SDECE have been watching you two ever since you arrived at Brie Comte Robert, Tony."

"Then why didn't they stop him leaving?"

"Because the only place they want him is back in Argentina. The French want this one nailed down tight. It never happened, understand me?"

"Of course, sir," Tony Villiers said. "Just another of my regular nightmares."

"I presume he's gone back to play hero again?"

"Something like that."

"Ah, well, that's no longer our concern. There is one more rather important item I'd like you to handle for me, Tony. It concerns Gabrielle. My information is that she'll be back in Paris tonight."

"What is it, sir?"

"You see, Tony, right in the middle of things, she started to crack, as you know. Wanted out, remember?"

"So?" Villiers said and suddenly his stomach was empty as if he knew by instinct that it was going to be bad.

"I needed to do something drastic to pull her together, so I told her that Richard was missing in action, believed dead."

"You mean it wasn't true?" Villiers said.

"He's fine, according to my latest information," Ferguson said. "Still in the thick of it, of course."

"You fucking bastard," Villiers said and slammed down the phone.

He started to run across the concourse toward the

gate into the international departure lounge and then slowed to a halt. Too late to catch Montera now. Far too late. He turned wearily and moved toward the main doors, wondering what on earth he was going to say to Gabrielle.

16

On the terrace of the big house above the Rio de la Plata outside Buenos Aires, Donna Elena Llorca de Montera interrupted her embroidering when a maid announced, "There is a lady to see you, Donna Elena. A French lady. Señorita Legrand."

Elena de Montera said calmly, "Please show her in."

Gabrielle paused in the Frencn windows, "Donna Elena?"

The old woman looked at her without expression. "Yes, I see exactly what he meant. You are beautiful."

"Where is he?" Gabrielle said. "I have something vital to tell him."

"Raul is at Rio Gallegos, flying with his squadron, or what's left of it. He loves you very much."

"I know that."

"So much that he discounts your activities for British Intelligence as being of no consequence. You know

Raul was deeply distressed by the fact of your brother's death."

"But they lied to me!" Gabrielle spread her hands. "My people lied to me, to keep me in line! Richard's alive and well."

"Mother of God." Elena de Montera put a hand to her eyes only for a moment. "Were you aware that my son had your name painted on the nose of his Skyhawk?"

"Yes," Gabrielle said.

"When he got back he had an extra word added. It now reads, Gabrielle Gone."

"I must see him," Gabrielle said. "I'll go to Rio Gallegos."

"My dear, it's a restricted military area. However, General Dozo, commander of our air force, is one of my dearest friends. Let's go inside and I'll make a phone call."

"If you only could," Gabrielle said.

She put an arm around Gabrielle's shoulder as they went in through the French windows. "Men, my love," she said, "are easy enough to handle as long as one understands their conceit."

It was just before four o'clock in the morning when Raul Montera moved across to the window of the operations room at Rio Gallegos and peered outside. It was pouring rain, the apron where the three Skyhawks waited awash with it as the ground crews worked on them in the light of the arc lamps.

The young pilots who were to fly with him filed

out and Montera turned, finishing the last of his tea. The room was quite empty now, only the chairs, the large-scale charts of the Falklands on the wall, the cigarette smoke. Someone had left a cigar burning on the edge of an ash tray. He stubbed it out carefully then picked up his helmet and went outside.

He was tired, more tired than he had ever been, at the final end of things in some strange way. He took a deep breath and started toward the planes as a staff car came around the corner and pulled up beside him. The door opened and Lami Dozo got out, pulling a greatcoat over his shoulders.

"Raul, how are you?"

"It could be worse. We lost another three yesterday. What you might call scraping the barrel."

Lami Dozo gave him a cigarette. "San Carlos again?"

"That's right."

"This could be the last one, Raul. The British have taken the high ground outside Port Stanley. We believe they've taken at least four hundred prisoners. I think it may only be a couple of days before Menendez will have to surrender."

"So—what was it all about?"

"I don't know," General Dozo said. "There were those, and I was not among them, who said we needed a war to prove ourselves. I hope the same people are now just as prepared to work for a new Argentina."

"But still we go on?"

"Yes, sometimes it is necessary."

"I often think of that uncle of mine, my mother's brother, the one who disgraced the family by fighting bulls. I remember as a young man watching him waiting, in his suit of lights, to enter the plaza at Mexico City, the trumpet sounding high and sweet, playing 'La Virgen de la Macarena.'" Montera smiled. "I feel like that rather a lot these days. As if the beast is waiting for me out there. My uncle didn't know when to stop either."

Lami Dozo looked grave. "This isn't good, Raul."

"Ah, but it is, General. You see, I've discovered the big secret. I don't actually care any more whether I live or die. That way, they don't know how to handle me, whoever *they* are up there."

"Raul, please," Dozo said.

"Not to worry. Two ears and a tail when I get back."

They gave each other the *abrazo*, the formal embrace, patting each other on the back.

Dozo said, "Before you go, there's someone very anxious to see you. Over there by the fence." He pointed and Montera saw a black limousine. "Go on, you haven't much time."

As Montera walked across to the high wire fence, a chauffeur got out of the car and opened the rear door and Donna Elena got out.

"Mama," Montera said in astonishment.

She smiled. "You look tired."

"I am tired." He smiled ruefully. "I suppose you're going to tell me I'm too old to play games."

"No, I haven't time. Instead, I've brought you a gift."

She turned back to the car, and Gabrielle got out and stood looking at him, pale in the yellow light of the arc lamps, a military raincoat someone had loaned her over her shoulders. For a moment only he was totally stunned and then he smiled that inimitable smile she knew so well.

"You look wonderful. Has anyone told you that lately?"

"No one I'd care to hear it from."

She moved close, taking in every detail of his appearance. The yellow flying suit, the shoulder holster, the helmet in his left hand, the tousled hair damp from the rain.

He said gravely, "But this isn't good. You shouldn't have come."

"There's no other place on earth where I should be," she said. "I'm not Gabrielle Gone, Raul, I'm Gabrielle here and Richard isn't dead. He's alive and well. They lied to me because I wanted out, don't you see?"

He stared at her, frowning and said softly, "Oh my God, what bastards they are." And then he laughed out loud and fastened his hand over hers. "I'll be back, understand me? I love you and I'll be back. Believe that."

He kissed her hand, turned, and ran toward the line of Skyhawks. Within a matter of minutes, the night was filled with the roaring of their engines. Donna Elena got out of the car and stood at Gabrielle's side as the planes taxied out one by one. A few moments later they started to take off, and shortly after that there was only the sound of them fading into the distance.

They swept in over the mountains of West Falkland as dawn came up, as close to the ground as they dared because of the missiles, and turned into Death Valley barely sixty feet above the water.

It happened incredibly fast as always. First the mountains, then Falkland Sound with the ships of the Task Force and more in San Carlos Water. Montera was aware of the Skyhawk on his right sinking desperately, a Rapier missile on his tail. There was an explosion, a ball of fire.

Montera banked, went in low through a ball of fire as the ships below opened up with everything they had. The Skyhawk shuddered as shrapnel pierced its body. Montera saw a frigate coming up fast, steadied the plane, took aim, released his bombs and climbed, banking and looking back. There were no explosions, and he laughed out loud at the nonsense of it all.

"Mother of God, even at this stage of the game they can't get the fuses right."

In the operations room at Rio Gallegos, Donna Elena and Gabrielle sat by the stove and Lami Dozo stood at the window, peering out at the rain in the gray dawn light, drinking coffee. A young lieutenant came in, saluted, and handed him a message. The general read it, nodded, and the lieutenant went out.

Donna Elena said, "You don't look happy, General. Is it bad news?"

"These days, what other kind of news is there?"

Raul Montera burst out of cloud at four thousand feet and, still descending, followed the other Skyhawk, which was going down fast, smoke pouring from it.

Montera, disregarding all procedure, called over the radio, "Come in, Enrico. How bad is it?"

There was no reply, and suddenly he saw a Sidewinder missile homing in on the damaged plane. He wished he could reach out and somehow stop it, but there was a sudden tongue of flame that mushroomed into a fireball as the Skyhawk disintegrated.

A Harrier, that's all it could be. What lousy luck, for they had almost reached the limit of the Harrier's radius for a sea chase. Montera corkscrewed instantly, the reflex of much combat experience, and saw the second Sidewinder spiraling madly away over on his right, a rogue missile, directional equipment haywire, plunging down toward the sea. The Harrier only carried two Sidewinders, which meant he now had only its 30-mm Aden cannons to contend with.

The Harrier swung in on his tail and Montera, banking, trying to escape, suddenly felt the impact of cannon shell. The cockpit canopy over his head disintegrated, and Montera felt two simultaneous violent blows as shrapnel tore into his left arm and leg.

The Harrier swung in again and then it was the dream, only this time for real, the eagle descending, claws reaching out to destroy, curving in on his tail to finish him off.

He was already down to a thousand feet and Gabrielle seemed to say in his ear what she had said the first time he'd had the dream in the flat in Kensington.

"Remember to drop your flaps. Eagles overshoot, too."

And Montera did just that. It was like running into a solid wall, and for a moment he thought he'd lost power completely. The Harrier pilot had to take violent evasive action to avoid a collision, climbing fast, and Montera seized his chance and went right down.

It was probably the most hazardous piece of flying he'd ever attempted as he leveled out at a hundred feet, for the wind was such that the sea was lifting in forty-foot swells.

He looked up for his adversary, saw him high overhead. There was a crackle of static and a voice said in English over his radio, "Good luck, whoever you are. You've earned it," and the Harrier, at the limit of its radius, banked away, turning back toward the Falklands.

Montera's Skyhawk came in low over the sea at five hundred feet, the wind whistling through the shattered cockpit. His face was smeared with blood from the many cuts caused by the disintegration of the canopy. He sat, hands frozen to the column, one arm and leg of his yellow flying suit now scarlet, a slight fixed smile on his face as he came into Rio Gallegos base.

"Gabrielle," he prayed aloud, "Don't let me fail now."

As the airfield came into view, the runway lights gleaming in the gray morning, Lami Dozo stood in the control tower, a pair of field glasses to his eyes.

Raul Montera's totally washed-out voice sounded over the radio loudspeaker. "No time for procedure. I'm bringing her straight in."

As Dozo watched, the Skyhawk brushed over the buildings at the north end of the runway and almost stalled. Montera was aware of the vehicles roaring out to meet him from the control buildings. He gave the Skyhawk a final burst of power and then let it down. It bounced back up again twice, and finally stayed, Montera trying to keep its nose pointed ahead as it swayed to the side, water from the rain-soaked runway spraying up in a great cloud, till it finally came to a stop.

He stayed there, head bowed, aware of voices and then careful hands lifting him from the cockpit. He opened his eyes, saw the faces, so many faces, Lami Dozo's amongst them.

He smiled. "Two ears and a tail, eh, General?" and then he passed out.

And so it was over. In Port Stanley the Argentines laid down their arms, and in Buenos Aires an outraged mob made it plain that Galtieri had to go. In London, at Westminster on the same day, the British

Prime Minister rose from her seat to tell the Members of Parliament assembled before her of the triumphant conclusion to one of the most astonishing feats of arms since World War Two.

At the Sisters of Mercy Hospital in Buenos Aires, Gabrielle and Donna Elena waited outside Montera's room. Finally, the door opened and the chief surgeon emerged. They stood up.

"Well?" Donna Elena demanded.

"Not good, but he'll survive. He'll certainly never be fit to fly a jet aircraft again. You may go in."

Gabrielle turned inquiringly and Donna Elena smiled. "I've got my son back. All the time in the world. You go in now. I'll wait."

When Gabrielle opened the door, she found him propped up against pillows, the cuts on his face stained purple with some preparation or other. His left arm was in a plaster cast and there was a cowl beneath the sheets to protect his injured leg.

She stood by the side of the bed without saying anything, and as if sensing her presence, he opened his eyes and smiled.

"You look awful," she said.

"I'll be all right. The surgeon told me I'll still be able to play the violin, and you know, that's really very amusing. You see, I can't play the violin."

And then she was laughing and crying at the same time, on her knees at the side of the bed, her face against his.

17

It was the finest of London mornings, the early winter sun shining on the hoarfrost on the trees in St. James's Park as the taxi drove up Pall Mall toward Buckingham Palace.

Tony Villiers was wearing the uniform of his regiment, razor sharp, the scarlet and blue dress cap with gold-rimmed peak, Sam Browne belt gleaming, medal ribbons in a neat row on the left breast.

The taxi driver said, "Big day, eh, gov'nor? Was you down there in the Falklands?"

"Yes," Villiers said.

"That's funny, guv. I didn't know the Grenadier Guards was there as well."

"One or two," Villiers told him.

The driver grinned in the mirror. "We showed 'em, didn't we?"

"Yes," Villiers said. "I suppose we did."

They rounded the Victoria monument and were cleared at the main gate where the taxi was allowed through into the courtyard. Villiers alighted and took out his wallet.

"Nothing doing, guv, have this one on me," the cabby said and drove away.

Villiers followed the people who were streaming in through the main doors of the palace. There were members of all three services, most of them accompanied by their nearest and dearest, the women wearing hats specially bought for the occasion.

There was a general air of gaiety and excitement, a real sense of occasion as they mounted the red-carpeted stairs and entered the picture gallery, where rows and rows of chairs waited, facing the raised platform in the center where the Queen would sit.

A military band played light music, there was a buzz of conversation as people took their seats and talked together in low voices. Each recipient of an award was allowed two guests at the ceremony, usually family. Villiers had no one.

He sat in the chair assigned to him by an usher and looked around him at the marble statues, the paintings on the wall, and the crowd waiting so expectantly, children among them, keyed up for the big moment.

The talking died away as the band started to play "God Save the Queen" and everyone stood as she walked in.

People had been formed up in ascending order of decoration, the Navy first as the senior service, then the Army, followed by the RAF. As each man's name was called, he went forward to receive, at the Queen's hands, his award and a few moments of conversation.

There were several other awards of the Distinguished Service Order that morning. When Villiers' turn came, he moved forward and stood there, waiting for the Queen to pin the medal to him.

She said, "Not much we can say about this one, Colonel Villiers."

"Major, ma'am."

She smiled again as she pinned the DSO in place. "You obviously haven't seen the Army List this morning."

And then Villiers was moving away, as the next recipient came forward.

He stood in the courtyard outside the palace at the bottom of the steps, and opened the box and looked at the medal again, then he slipped it into his pocket and crossed to the main gates. The constables on duty saluted him as he passed out and moved through the usual crowd of tourists. Here and there a camera clicked, but he took no notice, hesitated, then crossed from the monument, toward St. James's Park.

He paused to light a cigarette and a black Bentley slid in to the curb beside him, Harry Fox at the wheel.

The rear door opened and Ferguson looked out. "You're looking well, Tony. Big day."

"I suppose so," Villiers said.

"I hear Gabrielle married her colonel in Buenos Aires last month."

"I know," Villiers said. "She wrote to me."

Ferguson nodded. "You've heard about your promotion?"

"Yes."

"Good. Get in." Ferguson leaned back.

"What for?" Villiers asked him.

"My dear Tony, who do you think arranged your promotion? I did and not as a birthday treat, but because it suits my purposes, and I'd like to point out that the rank is only acting. Your regiment won't be at all pleased."

"You mean you've got a job for me?"

"Of course. Come on, boy, get in. I haven't got much time. I've a meeting at the Ministry of Defense at two o'clock."

For a wild moment, Villiers almost obeyed and then he remembered Gabrielle at Maison Blanc and the look on her face. *You're worth so much more than Ferguson and his dark games. You're worth a little joy,* that was what she'd said.

He shut the car door. As he turned away, Ferguson leaned out of the window. "What are you playing at, Tony? Where are you going?"

"For a walk in the park," Villiers said and turned across the grass through the trees.

The expression on Harry Fox's face was pure delight. "Looks like you've lost him, sir."

"Nonsense," Ferguson said. "He'll be back. Drive on, Harry."

He leaned back in the seat, took a file from his briefcase, and started to leaf through it as the Bentley moved out into the traffic.

Exciting SIGNET Fiction For Your Library